THE EXPAT'S GUIDE TO MANAGING YOUR MONEY

*Published with the support
and encouragement of*

KINGSTAR INSURANCE AGENCIES LLC.

THE EXPAT'S GUIDE TO
MANAGING YOUR
MONEY

ROBIN E WELLS

MOTIVATE
PUBLISHING

Published by Motivate Publishing

Dubai: PO Box 2331, Dubai, UAE
Tel: (+971) 4 282 4060, fax: (+971) 4 282 0428
e-mail: books@motivate.ae   www.booksarabia.com

Office 508, Building No 8, Dubai Media City, Dubai, UAE
Tel: (+971) 4 390 3550, fax: (+971) 4 390 4845

Abu Dhabi: PO Box 43072, Abu Dhabi, UAE
Tel: (+971) 2 677 2005, fax: (+971) 2 677 0124

London: Acre House, 11/15 William Road, London NW1 3ER
e-mail: motivateuk@motivate.ae

Directors: Obaid Humaid Al Tayer and Ian Fairservice

Edited by Jackie Nel and David Steele, assisted by Zelda Pinto

Designed by Fred Dittlau and Johnson Machado

First published 2004
Reprinted 2006

ISBN: 1 86063 147 9

British Library Cataloguing-in-Publication Data
A catalogue record for this book is available from the British Library

Printed and bound in the UAE by Rashid Printers, Ajman, UAE

Introduction

Thank you for buying this book. I hope it will prove to be the first of many good investments!

This is a book about financial planning for expats. It's been written to help you reach your goals, making you richer and more secure. I trust it will also educate and amuse you in the process.

As an expat, you face many differences in your new host country. With these differences, come opportunities – for growth, for learning, for adventure and for financial security. You have the chance to make your fortune faster now than you might have been able to do at home. In fact, for many of us, that was one of the appeals of becoming expatriate in the first place.

But being an expat has its own particular considerations when it comes to managing your money.

You'll have greater disposable income than your friends back home, an accelerated window of opportunity to build your assets, property is likely to be a major consideration – and you'll need to build your own safety net, since you will no longer be covered by the social security of home.

What all this means is that managing your money as an expat is different, just as driving a car or doing business is different. The rewards are potentially greater, but so are the risks. You may have 101 opportunities to build a secure future for you and your family, but there are a million ways to spoil it.

That's why I wrote this book. . . .

Whether you succeed or not is ultimately up to you. I can't change that. But if you are sincerely committed to getting the most out of your time offshore, this book is here to show you how to make the most of your money.

Contents

Chapter one

The principles of managing your money

Being successful in managing your money is not difficult or complicated. In fact it's quite simple.

It's not something that requires vast amounts of money to begin with either – you don't have to be wealthy to think about financial planning. Quite the opposite. We hope that when you've finished this book, you can put some of it into practice and achieve wealth and financial security.

However, while it's quite simple to manage your money well, this is not the same as saying it's always easy.

To manage your finances you'll need vision, discipline and commitment.

The first step in being successful is to have a clear picture of what it is you want to achieve. Then you have to find a way of turning that vision into reality. This requires careful planning.

Planning is the cornerstone of all successful investing or financial management – whether you're budgeting for the household expenses or creating a complex investment and tax strategy.

Before you start any activity, you need to plan and plan thoroughly. In this chapter, you'll begin by learning how to draw up your own financial plan.

Financial planning – your key to security

To make the most of your money as an expatriate, you'll need a financial plan.

This is a book about financial planning and how you, as

1

an expatriate, can learn to create a personalised plan that will meet your needs.

But what is a financial plan?

In simple terms, a financial plan is a commitment to build financial security. A good plan, put into practice, will protect you and maximize your use of money in the present while building security for you and your family in the future.

Many of us are interested in investment. This is understandable – investment is exciting and glamorous. This book will explain how you can make some sensible investments. But the wise investor is someone who sets goals and builds foundations before thinking about making money grow. This book shows you how to do both.

To help you create your own plan, we are going to look at two simple templates. These are basic guidelines that you can use in designing a plan that suits you.

The first will show you how to blend different financial needs as the building blocks in a coherent and logical plan. The second template shows the importance of time in your planning and knowing where you are upon your journey. By learning these two templates and blending them to suit your needs, you can create your own financial plan.

A hierarchy of needs

Different financial needs have different priorities. You need to consider some things before you consider others. This is a key part of building a successful and solid financial plan.

Rather like building a house, it is important that you complete the foundations of your financial plan before you proceed to the next stage. Like a house built on many levels, your plan needs to progress logically from one storey to the next. Trying to work on the attic or roof before you have completed the foundations is bound to end in disaster!

One way of looking at this is to think in terms of a hierarchy. In the same way that the sociologist Abraham Maslow suggested there was a hierarchy of human needs, so we suggest that there could be a hierarchy of financial needs. That is to say, you need to address the basic needs in your financial planning first before you can consider more complex issues.

In Maslow's model (right), human needs such as food, warmth, shelter, social recognition and spirituality tended to develop in a hierarchy, with each one becoming relevant only when the previous need has been satisfied.

Diagram 1.1: Maslow's hierarachy of needs.

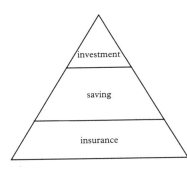

Diagram 1.2: A suggested hierarachy of financial needs.

Likewise, in our financial model (left), you should only address a new layer once the previous layer has been properly met.

The bottom level of your financial-needs hierarchy is comprised of insurance. The second level is concerned with setting aside current income so that you may enjoy it in the future. And the last level of the plan, perhaps the culmination of earlier work done in previous years, concerns investment of lump sums.

The point here is that you should sort out your basic priorities before trying to address more complicated issues: don't plan a complex investment strategy that consumes all your savings if you don't have your insurances in place or an emergency fund in a bank for unforeseen expenses.

3

Here is an example of what could happen if you didn't have a plan:

You are in a car accident. It wasn't your fault and you are (thank God!) alive but you have been injured. You need to pay the hospital bills. Because you didn't have medical insurance, this consumes all the money you had put aside in the bank. You're unable to work while you're in hospital, so your income ceases. After coming out of hospital you're told you cannot work for six months.

In order to feed yourself and pay your rent, you have to cash in the pension fund that you started two years ago. Then you have to undergo a further operation to fix your back, which still isn't completely healed. This consumes all the money you were planning to place into an investment portfolio, after months of painstaking research.

After only two months you have nothing, your savings are gone, you can't work, and you can't pay the rent. And your pet cat needs feeding.

Without a structure to your finances, it all collapses very quickly. The point is simple – don't try to do the clever stuff until you've sorted out the basics.

Each of these areas will be discussed in more detail in later chapters, but here's the sequence of the basic financial hierarchy:

Step one: Insurance
Step two: Allocating disposable income
Step three: Investing accumulated capital

You may have noticed that the structure of this book also follows this sequence – section one is entitled foundations, section two is about saving, and section three is all about investing.

Using this hierarchy model is a great way of starting your first financial plan. However, there is one thing missing: time!

Life is dynamic and our needs change as we grow. That is why it's also useful to overlay this first model with another template. . . .

The seven stages of life

"All the world's a stage", wrote Shakespeare in *As You Like It*, "and one man in his time plays many parts."

For Shakespeare, there were seven ages of man, from the infant "mewling and puking" to the old man, in his "second childishness and mere oblivion".

In financial planning, one of the key concepts with which to frame your plan is time. Life is dynamic, and your needs at one moment may be totally different from your needs at another point in your life. Things change. And so do you.

If you look at the diagram below, you will see that most peoples' lives tend to follow the same pattern. You go to school, you work, you get married, you have children, the children grow up, you retire and you die. Note also how your income rises, then falls, as you progress through life.

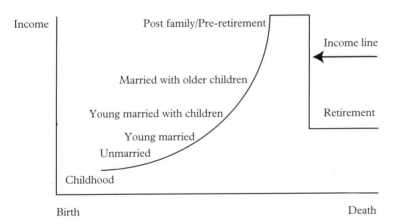

Diagram 1.3: The seven stages of life.

In each of these periods you'll have specific priorities that need to be addressed – either to protect yourself *against* something harmful happening in the here and now, or to ensure that something you desire *will* happen in the future.

5

Let's consider an example. If you are recently married and about to start a family, you will need to give serious thought to your life insurance (to ensure there is money to provide for your family if you were to die suddenly), and you may also wish to consider planning for your childrens' education, especially if you wish to educate them privately or send them to university. By contrast, if you were in your 70s, your priorities might be estate planning and mitigating tax, and the last thing on your mind would be an education fees plan!

A fuller explanation of each of these areas is provided in the following chapters, by the way, so don't worry if you're getting lost. The important thing to remember, for now, is the template and the way that your needs will change through time.

If we add some examples of typical needs to the seven stages of life, you can see the completed template on the opposite page.

So we've learnt that we should structure our affairs to resemble a pyramid, with insurance as the foundation, and that we should know where we are on the journey of life, and plan accordingly. Always track your progress on your plan and be ready to change it as your circumstances change.

It is up to you

Before you shoot off and make all sorts of plans, here are a few final pieces of advice that may prevent disappointment later on.

Take responsibility for your financial life. Take responsibility for getting started on a proper plan and take responsibility for putting it into action. Take responsibility for the consequences if you don't.

Secondly, have realistic expectations. If you do your homework, you'll understand a little more about the financial world and how things work. If you're buying insurance, read about it, check through the features and benefits of the programme you're selecting and make sure

THE PRINCIPLES OF MANAGING YOUR MONEY

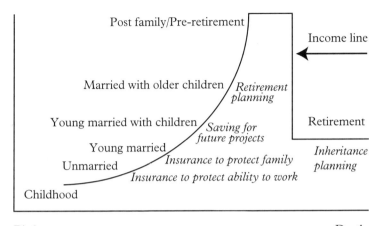

Diagram 1.4: The seven stages of life with typical financial planning needs.

you understand it. Make sure it meets your needs and that you know what to expect. If you are investing in the stock market, for your own sanity's sake, make sure you're being realistic in your expectations. The average market return from 1926 to the present day for the US stock market is about 9 per cent a year. You will not get 25 per cent a year every year, so don't build your dreams around it.

Thirdly, think about the tax consequences of what you do, and what you own. This doesn't mean obsessing about the tiniest differences between gross and net interest at your bank, but it does mean thinking through the serious projects you embark on in life. If you make serious investments, always check out the tax treatment in advance. This could apply as much to a portfolio of shares as it does to a holiday home in France. And, above all, take the time to mitigate inheritance or estate tax before you die – it is simple to do and saves a lot of heartache later.

Lastly, commit to action. The sooner you get started on your plan, the better.

7

Getting ready to start

Before we embark upon our plan, let's make sure we have a good starting position.

If you have any debt, try and clear it or at least make it manageable. In particular, you should try and reduce your dependence upon credit-card debt before drawing up your financial plan, just because that debt is preventing you from doing so many better things with your money.

A quick word about *credit cards*: they are a great invention and, used wisely, can really help your general financial management. The trouble is, credit cards are all too easily abused. To get the most out of your cards, without falling into the trap of long-term debt, you should clear your balance on a regular basis. If you have a large debt, set a target date by which you intend to bring the balance down to zero again.

Try to avoid paying just the minimum amount due on your card each month, as this is often carefully calculated to keep you servicing the same debt for the remainder of your working life. A balance of $4,500 on your credit card could take an estimated 44 years to pay-off if you just pay the "minimum amount due". And how much interest will you have paid over this timescale? About $17,000. . . .[1]

Finally, make an *income and expenditure* spreadsheet, and review it regularly. You will probably be horrified by how much you spend on 'stuff'! If you have not done this before, there is a template on the opposite page you can use.

If your expenditure outweighs income, you have some cutting back to do!

Starting your plan

To draw up your personalised financial plan, work out where you are in the seven stages model. Then work out what you need to do according to the hierarchy model.

---

[1] Source: The Motley Fool *Eight Commandments of Credit*, see www.fool.com

8

INCOME AND EXPENDITURE ANALYSIS

Income per month

Salary .... _____

Investment income .... _____

Any other income, eg rent .... _____

Total income .... ================

Expenditure per Month

Rent .... _____

Car loan/taxi fares .... _____

Insurances .... _____

Groceries .... _____

Telephone .... _____

Electricity and water bills .... _____

Eating out .... _____

Clothes .... _____

Childrens' school fees .... _____

Childrens' clothes .... _____

Petrol .... _____

Entertainment .... _____

Holidays .... _____

Property .... _____

Total expenditure .... ================

Difference: (+ or -) .... ================

Combine the two, and tailor it to suit yourself.

Remember, the following chapters will tell you more about each area, so start an overall structure now, and you can revise it as you go along.

But be sure that you establish a time-scale to get it up and running, and be sure that your plan allows sufficient flexibility to change as and when your circumstances change!

Now let us start our journey to financial security by learning about the foundation – insurance.

Section one

Foundations

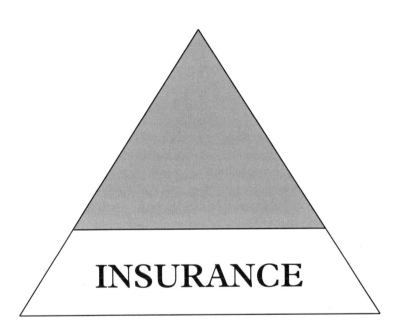

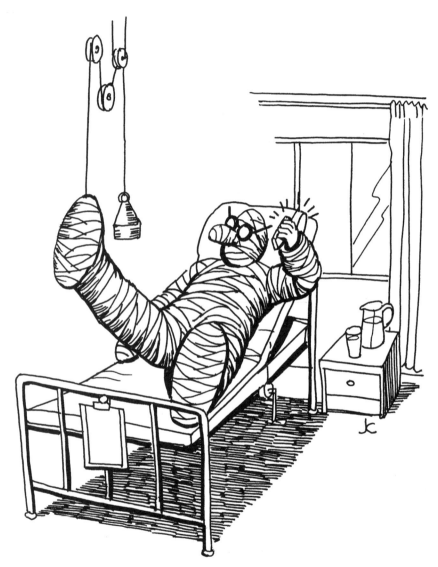

". . . Hello? Is it too late to buy a medical insurance plan?"

Chapter two

Insurance

If you heard about an asset that would provide you with around one-million dollars[1] over your lifetime, you might be interested. If you then learnt that this asset wouldn't cost you anything to buy, you'd be very interested. And if someone told you that you already possessed this asset but it could be lost at anytime, you'd want to protect it, wouldn't you?

So what is this amazing investment?

It's simple – it's you.

The best investment asset you have is your very own self. Your earnings capacity means that you'll produce more than any other investment asset you are ever likely to own or invest it. So, protect it. The wisest investors do.

Insurance, as mentioned in the previous chapter, is the foundation of good financial planning. When you have addressed your insurance, you can go ahead and make all sorts of clever plans to buy a yacht in five years or retire in 10, safe in the knowledge that all angles are covered. You, and your money, are protected.

However, there are a number of types of insurance and it's important to understand a little more about how they work, and which type is right for you. This will prevent you leaving yourself vulnerable on the one hand, or spending unnecessarily on the other.

This chapter will help you find what you need. We begin with life insurance.

---

[1] All references to dollars in this book refer to US dollars.

1. Life insurance

Most of us will have heard of life insurance.

And most of us will have some sort of vague notion that it's 'a good thing' and that we ought to have some. What we don't know is how much we may need, in what circumstances it's necessary, and what type is right for us.

The basic premise is simple. Life insurance pays out a specified amount in the event of your death. This money is paid into your estate – the combination of assets held by you at time of your death – or, and this is even better, to those persons you've nominated on your application when setting up the plan.

The types of life insurance

The two basic types of life insurance are term insurance and whole-of-life assurance. Let's look at these to see what they mean and which might be best for you.

As you might have guessed, term insurance provides you with cover for a specified period (the term), defined at the outset. If you die during this term, then the guaranteed death benefit (the sum assured) will pay out. If you don't, and you survive the term, then the plan ceases and nothing is returned to you. Let us repeat that point: nothing is returned to you and there is no value in the plan. This is insurance, pure and simple.

The other type of life insurance, whole-of-life assurance, lasts for your lifetime and will pay out upon your death, whenever that is. In this sort of plan there's usually a value built up during the period you're paying into it, so if you decide to stop or cash it in for whatever reason, there's usually some money in your pot.

Whole-of-life insurance will invariably be more expensive than simple term insurance because it will pay out on a certainty – that you will die at some time – rather than a possibility that you might die during a particular period.

14

When might I need life insurance?

At its most basic, you'll need life insurance when you want to leave a lump sum to meet a liability in the event of your death. A liability could be the financial requirements of a dependent, for example, or a debt you owe to someone.

Let's consider the most common situation where life insurance is used: a family.

Mr and Mrs Good have two children, aged five and three. Both parents should have life insurance on their lives to ensure the surviving partner has enough money to bring up the children if one of them should die and, if they both die, that there's a fund for the children.

Life insurance is necessary here because there is a liability, or a financial dependence on the part of the family, at the time of death. Traditionally, without Mr Good, the

15

breadwinner disappears and the family suffers a complete loss of monthly income. Without Mrs Good, there might not be anyone in the home to look after the children in which case, at the very least, Mr Good would have to change his work patterns or consider some hired help.

For a family then, life assurance on both adults is vital. In another instance, mortgage lenders will often require that you hold life insurance on your life if you are applying for a house loan. They will expect this insurance to be to the value of the loan they are giving you, and for it to last until your loan has been repaid. This reassures the mortgage company in the event of your death – if you are no longer around to pay back the loan, then the proceeds from the insurance will cover it and will allow your family to keep the house.

When might I use term insurance?

Term insurance is the cheapest and most basic form of life insurance. It's suitable when there's a known need for a set amount of cover over a specific period.

For example, many families choose to buy life insurance to protect their children until the children are felt to be financially independent – this is usually around 18 to 21 years of age.

In this instance, a term policy would be used and written upon the lives of the parents until the children reach the chosen age.

In another scenario, if you're taking out a loan, the lender might insist upon term insurance for the period of the loan, to the value of the amount due, on the lives of those taking the loan.

In summary, if you have dependents – or someone who will lose financially as a consequence of your death – and this dependency only lasts for a specified and known period, then term insurance is usually the most cost-effective option.

16

When might I use whole-of-life assurance?

Whole-of-life insurance, by contrast, lasts for the whole period of your life and will pay out on your death, whenever that might be.

On the face of it, this type of policy might appear to be a much better deal than term assurance since you're guaranteed a pay-out. What's more, if you need to stop the policy, you can cash it in and you'll get some money back – the longer you have been paying in, the more you're likely to get.

This works because the life insurance company diverts some of your premiums into a 'pot' that grows every year. It is this pot that helps fund your contributions later in life. If you wish to cash in the policy, whatever you get back comes out of this pot. However, if you do cash it in, you might not have any insurance any more. . . .

Whole-of-life plans are genuinely useful for people who want to build a secure base for their families and who want to mix their savings with insurance protection. They also come in very useful in later life, when it may be difficult to start a new insurance policy – if you have a whole-of-life policy, then the premiums you pay should remain the same for life and all the time your fund is building.

As mentioned before, though, because you are effectively buying insurance *and* a form of savings plan, you'll pay much more to have a whole-of-life plan than a simple term plan.

In summary, life insurance is there to cover a potential liability if you die, whether the result of an accident, natural causes or illness. It's a must for anyone with a family. For an expat with a family, it is simply irresponsible to go without it.

Where life insurance can't help, though, is in situations where you suffer a serious illness or accident, but don't die as a result. Without some financial help at this time,

17

things could be very difficult for you and your family. This is where critical-illness insurance can be very useful.

2. Critical-illness plans

Whereas life insurance has been with us for a long time, critical-illness insurance is a relatively recent development.

With the progress in medical science during the late 20th century, many previously terminal illnesses have become easily treatable in hospital. The net result is that patients are now surviving illnesses that would have killed them 50 years ago.

However, many of the patients have to go through a course of intensive and lengthy treatment and many of them will find that their lives have changed substantially as a result. The insurance industry responded by introducing critical-illness plans.

The premise behind the plan is simple – the lump-sum benefit (sum assured) will pay out if you are diagnosed as having one of a list of serious illnesses or conditions. Typically, this list will include Alzheimer's disease, Parkinson's disease, heart attack, stroke, cancer, kidney failure, paralysis, a coma and total and permanent disability.

When might I need critical-illness insurance?

We believe that critical-illness insurance is one of the most important insurances you can buy, and that everyone should consider investing in such a plan.

The lump-sum benefit is usually paid on, or soon after, diagnosis. Even if you survive and make a full recovery, you'll receive the promised amount. This helps meet the costs of medical treatment, for example, or replaces lost earnings or profits during that period. Alternatively, it may be used for home alterations or specialised equipment needed to modify your lifestyle following treatment. In any instance, a cash injection at a time like this will greatly

18

relieve the other burdens you have to deal with.

Usually, it's purchased as a stand-alone term contract. In this instance, you may wish it to cover you during your working life; to the age of 60, for example. Parents also take it out to cover them during their child-raising years, when a serious illness would really threaten the family's financial security.

Alternatively, if you were taking out a large loan, it would also make good sense to purchase a slice of critical-illness insurance to protect yourself, and those close to you, during this loan period. Sometimes it can be added into whole-of-life plans, where it's also very valuable because the benefit lasts for the whole of your life.

Critical-illness plans are usually good value and we recommend them unreservedly. The lump sum they pay could come in very useful at a difficult point in your life.

However, the funds from a critical illness plan will only go so far. If you're unable to work, and can't claim your regular salary, how will you pay the monthly bills? This is where income-replacement insurance plans can help.

3. Income-replacement insurance

Income-replacement plans will pay a replacement income for as long as you are unable to work, through illness or an accident. Whereas critical-illness plans will pay a lump sum, income-replacement plans are set up to pay a proportion of your regular income direct to you during your period of sickness.

For this reason, this insurance is also known as permanent health insurance in that it creates an income stream as if you were in permanent health.

Income replacement plans are only available as term-based plans. Since they are by definition linked to your period of earning a salary, they're usually taken out for a term corresponding to your usual working life – ie up to your retirement age.

The plans usually have a set deferment period. This is the time that must elapse before the benefit will begin to pay. If it's 13 weeks, for example, you must be unable to work because of an illness or accident for 13 weeks before the plan will start to pay out.

You are usually only able to claim a proportion of your salary – often no higher than 70 per cent. This is set by insurance companies to ensure they're not caught out by malingerers for whom it's is as cost effective to stay off work claiming the plan's benefits as it would be to return to work!

When might I need income-replacement insurance?

Back in our home countries, this sort of insurance is traditionally favoured by the self-employed. It provides them with a safety net that they often lack, working outside the security of company-sponsored schemes.

For expats, however, company schemes are often minimal and few states provide much in the way of social security for visiting labour. Therefore, income replacement insurance can be a very useful benefit for expats. If you were taking on significant and fixed obligations that depend on your receiving a monthly salary of $2,000 for example, it would make good sense to establish an income protection plan to cover this liability. If you enjoy your lifestyle and want to protect it – get some insurance!

Remember, the whole point of your insurance foundation is to ensure that any unforeseen circumstance can be dealt with and doesn't result in you taking money from your other assets. A little expenditure here could save a lot more later.

4. Medical insurance

This is the fourth, and last, of the key foundations for expats.

Medical insurance covers the cost of medical treatment

arising from treatable medical conditions, whether caused by an accident or sickness. It's there to pay hospital bills, so acts as a very useful adjunct to critical illness and income replacement insurance.

Most medical insurers will meet the costs of in-patient treatment as well as out-patient treatment. In-patient means where you're admitted to a hospital bed, whereas out-patient treatment refers to treatment or consultations provided without needing to stay overnight.

Many providers also offer benefits such as repatriation of mortal remains, in the event of your death, and emergency evacuation if you're in an inaccessible location, or need specialised treatment that can't be provided locally.

There are plenty of providers to choose from, and you'll probably find a mixture of local and international insurance firms wherever you are. International firms tend to offer a higher level of benefits and a greater amount of security for the international expat. Local firms will tend to be cheaper and have policies more geared to local or regional customers.

What should I look for in medical insurance?

To a degree, what you look for depends on what you're willing to pay. We'd recommend that you go for the best available plan within your budget and that you don't take risks with your health.

Certainly you should look for a policy that provides cover when you really need it – international emergencies, for example, and with no restrictions on where you can be treated. For this reason, it might be sensible to choose a plan with less emphasis on reimbursing you for coughs and colds and basic medicines, but with a higher level cover for those times when you really need emergency treatment.

You should look for a plan that will offer guaranteed insurability. This means that the insurance company can't refuse to renew your cover, regardless of how ill you

. . . medical insurance plans always carry some exclusions . . .

become during your life. Some companies price their products as annually renewable contracts – which may be cheaper – but imagine what would happen if they refuse to renew your plan when you're in the middle of a long course of hospital treatment for a potentially life-threatening condition? It can happen.

It is also useful if your insurance company is a member of the International Federation of Health Funds. This will help you transfer your policy from one insurance company to a participating member company in another country without having to go through the procedure of submitting a new application – which could result in loadings or restrictions to your cover. This is very useful for expats, particularly those who move around a lot. Members of the International Federation of Health Funds include Blue Cross Blue Shield in the US and Canada, PPP International and BUPA International from the UK, and Australia's MBF.

Generally, the underlying cost of insurance tends to be the same the world over, so you get what you pay for. If one company is offering what looks like a great product at a very low price, it might be that they do not pay their claims. Beware of deals that look too good to be true.

The reputable companies tend to cost the same and all will offer a range of benefits that can be tailored to suit you. Chose the one that meets your needs and pay the going rate.

Company schemes

Lastly, it makes sense to check what your employer offers before taking any individual action. You can find out what exactly you are covered for by talking to your human-resources department.

Many companies employing expatriates will offer a basic life insurance, perhaps two or three times your salary, and some sort of medical insurance. Be sure you understand exactly what's on offer and take time to talk to an independent expert if you feel the need.

Company benefits are very valuable. If you have life cover with your company, ask if you can extend it through the group scheme – this is a cheap way of obtaining extra life cover at discounted rates. You could also ask if you can add your dependents to it.

Remember, however, that your company benefits will cease when you leave the company. It is always sensible to consider having your own insurance plans as well as any company-sponsored plans – many of us forget about insurance when leaving employment (and yet this is often the time when we most need it) and it gets more and more difficult, and expensive, to obtain insurance the older you get. So, find out what you have, and supplement it with your own personal plans. Remember, it's unlikely that you will be working with your present company forever!

Where can I buy individual insurance plans?

Insurance plans have to be bought through an agent of an insurance company. Offshore, these will either be direct sales agents (who work only for that company) or independent advisers or brokers granted an agency with the insurance company, allowing them to sell their products.

Usually, there isn't any cost differential between the two and an independent adviser should be able to provide you with a wider range of choices.

It's also unlikely that you'll benefit from any price reduction if you approach the provider directly. In fact, a lot of insurance companies will only distribute their products through third-party sales channels, such as brokers.

Applying for insurance

Selecting and buying an insurance policy should be simple. Establish which broad type of policy is right for you, check any specific variations suitable for your particular circumstances, then do your market research. Find out who offers these products in your marketplace and which companies are willing to sell them to you. Insurers will have different target markets and may not have a product for every nationality.

You'll need to declare all relevant information on the form, and try to answer the questions as fully as possible. You may need to go for a medical check-up, which will be reviewed by the insurance company's medical officer to see if there are reasons why they might have to load your rates.

The insurers will impose a loading or restriction to the cover if they think you present an above-average health risk

24

– this means they'll come back to you with a higher quote for the contract being proposed, or a reduction in the benefits being offered. You can either accept or decline this.

Lastly, if your application is successful, you'll be sent a policy document, which sets out the insurance contract and lists your right to benefits. Keep this in a safe place, as it will need to be produced if you want to make a claim some time later. Alternatively, if you have bought insurance for a mortgage company to cover a house loan, you'll need to send the original to them, but you should always keep a copy for yourself.

In summary

We can't over emphasise the importance of insurance. It isn't particularly exciting, it's not very glamorous and you won't make money out of it – but it could really assist you when you need a helping hand.

To make sure you get the right insurance, we suggest the following plan of action:

1. Check what your employers provide and identify any shortfalls in cover.
2. Decide what you need by reviewing your own circumstances and those of your family.
3. Decide which insurance is needed right now, and what might be needed in the future.
4. Approach a number of different insurance providers to get quotes, either direct or using a qualified intermediary.
5. Ensure you understand what's covered by the plan and what is excluded – always ask to see the policy wording. Take independent advice if you need.

Now, with the foundation in place, we can go to work!

In the next four chapters, you'll learn a very simple trick that will help you have plenty of money in five, 10 or 20 years' time.

It's called saving.

Section two

Allocating disposable income

". . . Maybe its time we opened a bank account . . ."

Chapter three

An introduction to saving

Now that we've completed our foundations, we can move to the next level – how best to use our disposable income.

In this part of the book, we look at saving – why save, where to save and how to choose the different homes for our savings according to what we're trying to achieve. We look at the basic homes for our savings and then more sophisticated investments, such as mutual funds and stocks and shares.

Before looking at where to save, it would be useful to remind ourselves why we should think about saving at all.

This is particularly important for expats. Just as you'll have a greater opportunity to save than ever before, you will also find greater temptation to throw your money away. While many of us come offshore with good intentions, within a year or two we are hooked on the glamour and competition of modern consumerism – new cars, expensive furniture, and all those other things that we are persuaded we need, to keep up with the Joneses or the Al Ansari's next door!

In this chapter, we want to show you how to save, while still enjoying your life offshore. The key is to find a balance.

Deferring consumption

"If you want things to stay the same, you're going to have to make some changes."

The principle of saving is simple: what you don't consume now, you can consume later. This applies as much to food you store in the fridge as it does for money you put into the bank. The principle is the same.

For some people, putting off consumption in the present is difficult. They might want to have it all now – and let the future look after itself. This is fine, in theory, but how many times have you found yourself wishing: "if only I'd kept that," or "if only I had saved a bit of money rather than spending it all"?

We don't know what the future holds for us, but past experience will show that it's always sensible to keep something aside as a reserve.

Of course, this can mean varying degrees of sacrifice, or even pain. If you're going to consume in the future, you have to accept that you can't have it all now. Some people never accept this, and live their lives in the perpetual present – until the money runs out and they become really miserable.

At the same time, we don't advocate avarice, where all expenditure is bad. That isn't much of a life and, if you were to die tomorrow, it would be a bit of a waste wouldn't it?

The key thing is to find a balance that suits you. Accept that if you want to live well in the future, you'll have to set aside something now. You will thank yourself later.

Where to save?

We know that saving is good, then.

The question is, though, where should we save? Should we put it all into the bank, or buy shares? Should we invest in property or start a savings plan? Or, why not keep it under the mattress in our bedroom?

The way to answer these questions is simple: ask yourself what you want to achieve.

If we're saving money, most of us would like to achieve some sort of return on that money – we want growth. However, we would also like to know that we can access our money. And, for most of us, we don't like to take risks – we don't want to see our hard-earned money drop in value, or disappear altogether.

So, there are three key considerations behind our

decision of where to save: growth, accessibility and security. But is there one home for your money that can provide all of this?

Well, let's consider some of the options. If you were to keep all your savings under your mattress, you would certainly have instant accessibility, and this probably wouldn't be very risky, but would you achieve growth?

No, of course not.

On the other hand, buying into stocks and shares might give you great potential for growth, but is your money accessible (not really) and are you prepared to accept the risks that shares can represent? Particularly if all your money were tied up this way?

Again, no.

The fact is, there is no one home for your money that will meet all of your needs. No asset provides the best possible growth, with complete accessibility and zero risk.

So, you have to find a balance. Better still, you should save different amounts of money in different types of asset according to their purpose.

What this means is that, to successfully manage your money, you could have one pot of your savings in one asset, such as the bank, another pot somewhere else, such as a fixed-term deposit account, some in a regular savings plan and some in a retirement account, each according to your plans for that money.

This way, you're getting the best of what each home can offer, without imposing the negatives of each onto all of your money.

How to do this is simple. Establish your goals and set your timescales according to the principles explained in chapter one. Then, divide your immediate savings objectives into three different boxes – short term needs, medium-term needs and long-term goals.

In the next three chapters we'll look at each of these in detail. But first, some basic pointers.

How much should I save?

What you get back is determined by what you put away. There's no point in blaming a tiny retirement fund on poor investment performance if all you've ever done is save $25 a month for 10 years. In any savings project, investment growth will rarely be more than your actual contribution: what's important is that you commit to putting money away, then you can think about where and how to allocate.

The first place to start, then, is to remove growth from the picture. Treat growth as a bonus. Instead, look at what you need to save for your various goals on the assumption there'll be no growth – then you can factor in the growth prospects of the relevant asset class, and see it as an added bonus.

So, calculate what you need, then work out how long you have to achieve this goal.

For example, if you need to have $10,000 saved in four years' time for a house deposit, it means putting away $208.33 per month for four years, without any growth. Factor in the growth after you have worked out the capital contribution.

The shorter the timescale, the less growth there's likely to be. A short timescale means you can't afford to take risks, which means you'll probably favour a safe harbour, such as banks or interest-paying deposits, where the growth potential is that much lower. Also, a short time-scale does not give much time for interest to build upon interest (known as compounding).

The longer the time-scale, by contrast, the more growth there's likely to be. This is because you're allowing time for the growth to compound and because you're likely to be invested in longer-term assets, which tend to repay their higher volatility with better overall returns over time.

Which brings us to a key basic truth. . . .

Rewards demand risk

Most of us, particularly investors, are after growth. But growth on your money often requires some amount of speculation: getting rewards means taking some risks. And, given the way the markets work, this reward can take time to come through. So, a useful formula to remember is this: Reward is determined by risk which demands time.

Reward

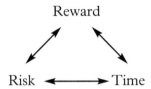

Risk ◄──────► Time

We'll come back to this in later chapters, but it's a key lesson to learn before embarking on any savings projects – reward is determined by risk which demands time.

Once you've understood this lesson, you can allocate your disposable income accordingly.

Get Saving!

As a summary, follow these key points:
1. Understand that having anything at all in the future requires a commitment to saving . . . now.
2. Understand that different savings needs, or different time horizons, require different homes.
3. Allocate into short-, medium- and long-term boxes.
4. Draw up initial savings projections without adding growth assumptions.
5. Understand that growth will be determined by risk and time.

In the following chapter, we'll make some initial suggestions on first homes for your money. This is where you should start your journey of saving and investing.

Chapter four

First homes for your money

We saw in the previous chapter that saving means putting money aside and allocating it to a number of different homes. And the choice of each home is determined by our plans for that money and our attitude towards risk, reward and time. Let's begin by looking at banks.

Banks are the first home for your money. Generally speaking, banks are safe, they pay interest and you have access to your funds when you need them.

Because they are accessible, low-risk and offer defined returns, banks offer an ideal home for emergency savings. This is the pot of money set aside for any unforeseen event and which needs to be easily accessible. By offering interest, the bank offers an advantage over keeping your money under the mattress and there's no risk of losing this money if the stock market falls (and banks tend to be insured against robberies!). So, your emergency fund – your 'cash buffer' – should always be held in a bank account.

This is the first home for your savings.

How much should I allocate to my cash buffer?

The purpose of this emergency money is to provide a buffer in case of an unforeseen event. A common example would be a change in jobs and the subsequent period without income. At a time like this, you'll greatly appreciate the little comfort cushion you'd built up at the bank.

On the other hand, because your bank account won't really offer you much potential for significant growth on your money, you don't want to keep all your savings there.

As a general guide, try to have between three and six

Banks are generally a safe place for your money . . .

months' living costs covered by your emergency funds. Depending upon your risk profile, you may wish to have more, but we wouldn't recommend any less.

How does interest benefit me?

Banks exist by lending your money to other people, often for business loans, home loans or personal loans. The interest rate charged to people receiving these loans is higher than the interest the banks give you on your money – this is how they make their money![1]

Interest varies from time to time, and from bank to bank. So it pays to shop around when choosing the bank for your savings and to keep any eye on the rates.

As well as accessibility and security, then, interest is a key benefit of keeping your money in the bank.

However, interest doesn't always mean growth. There's one important factor that can seriously reduce the benefits of keeping money in the bank for the long term – inflation.

Inflation is the rise in the prices of goods. Each year, as

---

[1] An emerging exception to this, particularly in the Middle East, is Islamic banking. Instead of paying interest, these banks reward depositors with a share of proceeds derived from cost-plus financing, which is generally held to be in accordance with Islamic *sharia* principles.

37

more and more people buy goods, manufacturers tend to put up their prices – so things become more expensive. And so the circle continues. This is the rise, or inflation, of living costs.

The interest rates given by commercial banks tend to follow the official rate proposed by the central bank of that particular country. And one of the roles of a central bank is to try and control inflation. So, when inflation is high, interest rates also tend to be high. When inflation is low, interest rates tend to be low.

What this means in effect is that bank accounts rarely give any real growth on your money. If your money is gaining an interest rate that's about the same as the rate of inflation, it isn't really growing at all. What's being given in interest is being taken away by the decrease in the purchasing power of your money.

For example, in the 1970s, inflation was high in many places around the world. Consumers were receiving 10 or even 15 per cent interest on their bank accounts, but because inflation was also 10 or 15 per cent, their savings weren't growing at all! Your money, in real terms, was running to stand still.

So, instant-access bank accounts are really only useful for short-term or emergency money.

Notice accounts

If you can afford to lock your money away for a period of time, the chances are that you'll benefit from better rates of interest. Notice accounts, for example, offer better returns than current accounts.

Banks and building societies offer a variety of notice accounts such as 90-day, call accounts, or 'blocked' accounts. The principle is the same: you specify a fixed period of time during which you agree not to withdraw your money. Because the bank has your money, and knows that it will have that money for a set period of time, it will reward you with more interest.

If you do withdraw before the end of the agreed term, you may face an interest penalty – often the bank will not pay the higher interest rate, but the current account rate, or you may have to accept a fixed penalty of, say, one per cent interest.

In many instances, higher interest accounts are a good solution. You know how long your money will be locked away, and you know in advance what return you'll get. In particular, when you don't want, or can't afford, to take risks with your money, they're ideal places to keep your savings.

For some investors, however, the returns offered by notice accounts are not sufficient. They want greater returns and are prepared to look outside the banks to find better returns. They look instead at bonds.

Bonds

As the name suggests, a bond is a form of promise. Only this time, rather than a bank giving the promise, it's a government or a company. In both cases, you're being rewarded for depositing your cash with an institution that will use it for its own projects.

When a government wants to raise money, it will issue a bond. You give your money to the government and in return it issues you with a bond certificate. By 'purchasing' the bond, you're lending the government whatever money you've paid, which they can then use to finance national projects such as roads or schools.

The government issues you with a bond, or promise, that they will pay you x per cent interest every year for as long as they have your money. Each bond will also specify the date at which the government promises to return your original investment to you. This is known as the maturity date.

So, with a bond, you get a specified interest rate each year and the promise to have your original capital returned in full at a specified date.

In America, government bonds are also called treasury bills, or T-bills. In the United Kingdom, they are often referred to as gilts, because the original government-bond certificate was issued on gold (gilt)-edged paper.

So, when you see the business news on television talking about the 30-year T-bill paying three per cent, this means that the US Government will pay an interest of three per cent every year if you invest in Treasury Bills, and will return your original investment in 30 years' time.

Corporate bonds

Like governments, companies also need to raise cash to finance expansion or fund the development of a new product.

And like governments, many companies choose to do this by issuing bonds – in this case known as corporate bonds.

Bonds tend to be rated according to the financial stability of the institution making the promise, whether it's a government or a company. These ratings tell you how sure you can be that you'll receive what is due to you. In general, governments tend to be stronger than companies, but not necessarily – corporate bonds issued by a stable multi-national such as General Electric, for example, may in fact be rated as safer than the government bonds of a small developing country.

The role of bonds in financial planning

Bonds are very useful in that they pay a regular, and predictable, income.

In comparison with other liquid assets, bonds occupy the middle ground between cash and shares. They tend to pay a higher overall return than simply holding your money on deposit in a bank, but will under-perform shares in the long run.

As you'd expect, bonds may be riskier than cash deposits, because there's the possibility that the company

40

or government paying your regular income might fail. As we're beginning to see, the more risk you're willing to take with your choice of assets, the greater the possibility that you'll receive higher returns.

In practise, it is rare for individuals to hold bonds directly. Bonds tend to be held as part of a managed portfolio run by professional money managers, in line with the overall strategy for obtaining returns on their clients' money.

In such portfolios, or managed funds, you'll find a blend of different assets, usually cash, bonds and shares. In this chapter, we've looked at cash and bonds. In the next chapter, we will look at managed funds, and introduce you to the benefits of investment based on shares.

Chapter five

Saving into funds

In the previous chapter we looked at the basic principles of saving and some of the first homes for your money. If you recall, you should save your money according to when you might need to access it. Try and create boxes for the short, medium and long term.

Cash, held in a bank account, is ideally suited as a short-term investment. It's instantly accessible, there's little risk or variability of returns, and you can be sure it will be there when you need it.

In this chapter, we'll look at medium-term savings projects and the vehicles you should consider for them. These are primarily managed investments, which are suited for longer-term goals because they give higher overall growth but may need time for this growth to come through.

These types of investments, typically managed funds, are suitable for medium- to long-term saving – from five years upwards. And, as we'll see, the longer, the better.

Managed funds

Managed funds are professionally-managed vehicles suitable for medium- to long-term saving and investment.

A managed fund is a pool of investors' money, which has been collected by a professional money manager and invested in a broad range of assets in the hope of gaining a reasonable return on that money. By giving your money to a professional money manager, the idea is that you achieve better results than if you were to try and invest it yourself.

The fund is usually managed and marketed by a

financial institution, such as a bank or investment house. They collect money from clients, who have chosen them to manage their money, and invest it as they see fit, according to their stated aims.

Sometimes they do very well; other times, not so well.

The fund managers make their money by entry fees and annual management fees.

Every time you put some of your money into their hands to be managed, they'll take a small initial percentage of the amount going in (some of this may also go to a broker or adviser who recommended the particular fund), and they'll take a further amount, usually between one and two per cent each year, as reimbursement for managing your money.

Managed funds accept money from regular savers and lump-sum investors (see chapter eight). In America, and increasingly around the world, managed funds are known as mutual funds.

The benefits of managed funds

In the previous chapter, we looked at cash and bonds as first homes for your money. One of the key benefits of managed funds is that they invest in both of these but also in something else – shares.

By investing in shares, also called stocks or equities, fund managers buy into companies around the world, and thus *share* in their fortunes. If the company does well, your money

Asset class	Nominal returns	Real returns after inflation at 3.6% pa
Shares	9.89%	6%
Bonds	4.85%	1%
Cash	3.86%	0%

Diagram 5:1: Table showing nominal and real returns of shares, bonds and cash during the period 1900–2002 [1]

does well. And sometimes they can do very well indeed – historically, the returns achieved by shares have outperformed both cash and bonds by a good margin (see diagram 5:1).

So, if you want to achieve real growth on your money, you have to be in shares.

But shares can be a risky proposition for the novice – look at the diagram below - and they can be difficult to get into on a do-it-yourself basis, either for reasons of initial outlay, time, knowledge or even inclination.

Asset class	Worst three-year loss during the period 1900–2002
Shares	60%
Bonds	25%
Cash	0%

Diagram 5.2: Table showing the worst three-year losing period for each asset class during the period 1900–2002[2]

For most of us, though, managed funds are a good way of harnessing the growth potential of shares without the potential drawbacks they bring.

And because the fund manager spreads your money across a wide range of different assets, they're a very good way of diversifying your assets, which reduces your overall risk.

How do managed funds fit into my financial plan?

First of all, managed funds are a medium- to long-term asset. They should be held as part of your medium- and/or long-term savings boxes, and can be very useful in your investment box.

[1&2] Source: *Bernstein, L,* The Four Pillars of Investing, *2002*

Remembering our formula of *risk determines reward demands time*, managed funds can outperform other assets such as cash and bonds but will need time for this to happen. They may also involve more middlemen than other assets – from the person who manages your fund to the person who recommended it to you – and each will add their costs. So, it will also take time for the growth to outweigh the costs associated with getting into funds.

Managed funds should be used where:

1. You can afford to wait *at least* five years before needing the money – and your time-scale will affect which type of fund you choose.
2. You can wait for the costs associated with getting into the funds to be overtaken by the growth.
3. You can accept that, on the journey to your goal, your money might periodically drop in value as well as rising.

So, going back to our financial plan, once you've achieved your basic emergency buffer fund in the Bank, and are ready to start saving on a regular basis for the medium- to long-term, managed funds are a good place to start.

But how do you get into them?

Where to find managed funds

Recent estimates indicate that there are some 33,000 managed funds available worldwide. Many of these will accept regular savings.

You can find funds advertised almost everywhere you look, from financial magazines to television. You may also wish to enlist the opinions of a financial adviser, but be aware that this person will have his or her own agenda, which may or may not fit in with yours!

Your success with your chosen fund will be determined by the following four factors. It is worth looking at each one in turn: Performance, Risk, Costs, Lock-ins.

Managed funds – performance

For most of us, performance is the key factor in choosing a managed fund. Indeed, it's the main reason to consider managed funds in the first place, knowing that they tend to outperform other assets over time. If it weren't for the possibility of better returns, we might as well keep all our savings in the bank, where we can at least be sure where they are!

But what do we mean by performance, how do we judge it, how can we find it and what is the price we have to pay to achieve it?

All fund companies want you to buy their funds. It's how they make their money – the more they have under management, they more fees they earn. So each fund company will produce data showing how well they've performed against their peers. They will tend to show how much the fund grew by last year (in percentage terms, for example, 5.5 per cent), what the overall growth has been over the last three and five years, and what the annualised growth would have been over that time, for example an average 9.8 per cent a year.

By the way, the best place to look for this data is in an independent ratings guide, rather than in the company's own literature, as each company tends to manipulate the facts somewhat to show their funds in the best possible light.

What you're looking for is a fund that's performed well, regularly – and over a reasonable period of time. Don't try to pick the best fund – stellar performance is rarely repeated – but do go for something that's consistently been in the top rankings of its sector.

The most common expectation of a managed fund is somewhere between eight and 10 per cent a year over a ten- to twenty-year time period. Naturally, funds vary and so do their respective performances but, as a rule of thumb, and in order to make investing in funds worthwhile, this is what you could legitimately expect to receive. Any more is a bonus.

47

But do remember this. Even if a fund has returned an average 9.8 per cent a year during the past five years, this is not to say that it's has returned this figure every year. Because managed funds can fall as well as rise in value, the returns may have been fantastic for one year and then awful thereafter, but still *averaged* 9.8 per cent a year during a five-year period.

Consider the diagram below and ask yourself which fund you would rather invest in - A or B?

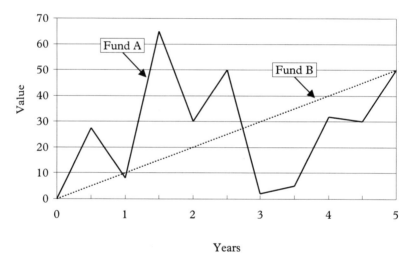

Diagram 5.3: Shows volatile fund (A) versus smooth fund (B), both achieving same average return during a five-year period.

What you need to look for, as well as the absolute figures, is the manner in which that return was achieved. Was it a smooth, steady growth, or an extremely volatile zig-zag? In essence, what you need to consider is the pattern of growth as well as the figures of absolute growth.

And whether or not you'll still want to buy into this fund once you've seen this pattern has a lot to do with your tolerance for risk.

Managed funds – risk

Managed funds do carry greater risk than cash or bonds. The value of your investments will fall as well as rise. This is a fact. If you can't handle this, then don't invest in managed funds. It's that simple.

But what do we mean by risk?

In this sense, assuming that you have bought a *bona fide* fund and haven't been misled over anything about it, risk means the variability of returns. It means that you might wake up one day and find that the fund into which you're putting your savings has dropped by 30 per cent in value.

". . . our fund managers use the most advanced stock-picking strategies . . ."

49

Of course, if that's the day you needed to access your money, then the risk has been real – you've lost out. Most of the time though, and assuming that we've allocated correctly to our time horizons, the day-to-day variability of returns is a hypothetical risk – you would only have 'lost money' if you need to cash out on that particular day. Otherwise, you simply wait for it to grow again.

A risky fund, then, is a fund where the value rises and falls quite dramatically.

There are two problems with variable returns. The first is that you might need your money on that day when the fund has dropped in value. That's why we have stressed the importance of keeping your money in different boxes with different time horizons.

The second problem is actually more to do with psychology. Nobody likes to feel they've bought a loser, so the psychological impulse to sell your fund after it's dropped by 30 per cent is enormous. This is the real danger of variable returns: whether or not you have the emotional stability to stay invested. The risk is that you sell out of the fund here, at its very bottom, not because you need to, but because you got scared.

By choosing managed funds, you are getting into investments that fluctuate in value – sometimes you're up and sometimes you're down. But, managed funds (being based around equities) do tend to outperform other assets over time. So, if you can deal with the ups and downs emotionally and if you've allocated correctly so you don't need this money when there's a chance it's in a dip, you should come out ahead.

And there's one remarkable saving grace when you invest on a regular basis. One of the beauties of regular saving is that you can use this volatility to your advantage. Simply put, there's a way that you can actually make more money by investing in volatile funds, rather than smooth-return funds. We'll show you how at the end of this chapter.

50

Managed funds – cost

Much of the above is out of your control. But you do have control over the various costs associated with your fund, and here it really does pay to shop around.

If you remember, managed funds make money for their providers by generating fees. Every time you put your money into the fund a percentage will be taken off. This is called an initial charge (or a bid/offer spread) and goes some way towards covering the costs of running and marketing the fund.

Getting into the markets isn't cheap. Historically, most managed funds will have an initial charge of up to five per cent. This is the price of admission. It means that up to five per cent of your investment, every time you put money into the fund, is eaten up as a charge.

Then, you need to remember the annual management charge as well. This is remuneration taken by the fund manager for the job of looking after your money. It is usually one to two per cent of the amount you have under management.

There *are* cheaper ways into managed funds. Many providers now offer no-load funds, which have low or no initial charges (but may hit you when you come out!). Others still will pay the fund manager performance-related fees rather than a fixed annual-management charge – the idea being that he or she is then motivated to perform better.

Alternatively, you could consider index funds. These are collective investment vehicles just like managed funds but they don't use fund managers, preferring to simply follow an index instead. We'll look at index funds more in chapter 10.

So, there's no reason why you should be paying over the odds to get into a fund. Many are just as good as the next, so controlling your costs can make a real difference to your overall returns. But don't base your decision purely on cost – the fund also has to have a good track record and some evidence of financial stability for it to be a worthwhile investment.

51

Managed funds – lock-ins

One last area of importance is the flexibility of your regular investment. Many funds, promoted on their own, have no lock-in whatsoever. You simply put in what you want on a regular basis and, when you want to stop, you can do so with no penalties. You can access your money when you like.

However, many managed funds are distributed through mutual or life companies as part of packaged savings products. These often have fixed-savings terms and you are supposed to complete the selected savings term.

This means that if you choose to take out a five-year savings plan, you should make every payment over the five-year term. If you don't, your overall returns may be diminished by penalties, or increased charges may eat into your growth. Sometimes these are not too substantial, and are offset by special offers or bonuses, but it pays to be aware of all the charges and conditions.

Contractual-savings plans such as these have their uses. They can be good for people with little financial discipline, for whom the threat of penalties or increased charges is a deterrent against missing a payment or accessing the money before the end of the term. They also often provide extra insurance benefits, such as life or serious illness insurance during the savings term, which can make them useful for specific savings projects (such as education fees, discussed at the end of this chapter).

However, it's always worth checking to see if there are any contractual obligations with the fund you're thinking of getting into. At the end of the day, it's still a case of buyer beware – and remembering to read the small print!

Dollar cost averaging

We referred earlier to the one saving grace of volatility. If there was ever a case for regular saving into managed funds, this would be it.

52

As we've seen, managed funds offer two key advantages over other asset classes for the medium- to long-term saver. They give you diversification, which reduces your risk, and are invested heavily in shares, which increases the potential for greater growth.

But even still, there may be some of us who are put off by the notion of investments falling as well as rising. We hear the shock stories in the media, the suicidal hysteria of a market crash, the people who lost everything . . . and no wonder some of us don't start saving until it's too late!

In reality, dollar cost averaging shows that market volatility can sometimes help regular savers over the long term.

In essence, it's simple. Imagine being given $10 to go to the fruit market every weekend and told to buy as many oranges as you can. At the end of each month, there's a sale. When there's a sale, the price of the oranges is marked down, so you can buy more oranges with your $10 than when the price is at its usual level. At the end of the year, you've actually accumulated more oranges because of these temporary drops in price than you would have if the price had remained level throughout the year.

What this shows us is that temporary drops in price allow us to accumulate more of an asset if we're spending the same amount on a regular basis.

And so it is with regular investing in funds.

By buying into managed funds on a regular basis, investors will lessen the risk of investing on one particular date when the prices are very high. A regular contribution into a fund will buy a varying number of units each month as the unit prices (the price of each share in the fund) fluctuate with normal market movements. When prices are low the contribution buys more units, and when prices rise it will buy fewer. This means that, over time, the average cost per unit will be less than the average unit price, because you've bought proportionally more units when prices were low.

Because of this, monies invested in funds that endure a period of volatility will actually outperform money in

53

steady-growth funds, since you're buying more when the price is low. Compare the performance of Fund A with Fund B in diagram 5.4 below.

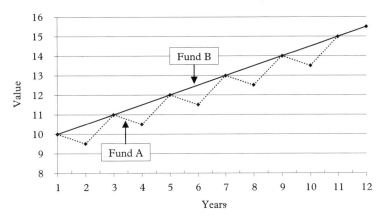

	Fund A	Fund B
Total Units purchased	990	953
Total cost of buying units	$ 12,000	$ 12,000
Market Value	$ 15,345	$ 14,771.5
% growth	28%	23%

Diagram 5.4: Benefits of dollar-cost averaging by investing in a fluctuating asset.

So, if you're planning for the longer term, you can afford to be aggressive and take risks. Remember that the risk is only made real if you actually need that money at that particular time.

Using managed funds for university or school-fees planning

Managed funds can also be ideal for education-fees planning, where the timescale is in the medium to long term.

For many expats, the education of their children is of

prime importance. Perhaps they are not eligible for state-sponsored education systems, or they'd like to give their children the headstart that only private schooling and university can offer. Either way, investing in your childrens' education is a wonderful thing to do.

But very few of us plan for it correctly. This is a shame as a little bit of foresight now could actually save money, as well as heartache, later.

Let's look at how this should be done.

First of all, we establish a payments schedule. This is the known cost of the education fees when they fall due in the future. Let's assume that we have two children, Asha (aged four) and James (aged two), and that we want to send them both to an international university to do their first degrees from the age of 18. Having checked the prospectus, we know that our preferred university will cost $20,000 each year at current prices.

A payments schedule may look like this:

Child 1	Child 2	Year	Fees (now)
Asha		2018	20,000
Asha		2019	20,000
Asha	James	2020	40,000
	James	2021	20,000
	James	2022	20,000
Total			120,000

Diagram 5.5: Schools fees table, current costs for two children.

The next step is to allow for inflation on the university fees. Like all things in life, we know that the university will put its fees up each year to keep pace with inflation. So we apply an inflation index (say, for example, three per cent a year) to the fees over the saving period (see diagram 5.6 on the following page).

We now know that we have to pay the following amounts of money at the following points in the future:

First child's name	Second child's name	Schooling year	Current cost of school fees	Adjusted to allow for 3% inflation
Asha		2018	20000	29,371
Asha		2019	20000	30,252
Asha	James	2020	40000	62,320
	James	2021	20000	32,094
	James	2022	20000	33,057
Total			120,000	187,094

Diagram 5.6: Schools fees table, adjusted to allow for the effects of inflation over the time period.

$29,371 in 2016, $30,252 in 2017, $62,319 in 2018, $32,094 in 2019 and $33,057 in 2020.

The final step is to work backwards and calculate what we need to set aside now in order to meet this liability in the future. And remember, start without including investment growth then factor it in at the later stage.

You can calculate this either by trial and error, or by developing a spreadsheet programme such as Microsoft Excel and using 'Goal Seek'. If you need help, this might a good time to find a qualified financial planner!

This will tell you the net amount you'll need to invest, without taking into account any growth on your money. If you now factor-in an assumed investment growth of, for example, 8 per cent a year, you can see how much you'll need to contribute each year.

This will almost certainly be less than if you had to pay the fees out of income as and when they fell due. In our example shown opposite in diagram 5.7, a total school fees bill of $187,092 is paid through contributions of only $95,692.

Not Bad!

You will see how it pays to plan ahead. And with the savings you've made, you can treat yourselves to a holiday – after all, you won't have to worry about the children any more.

Period from present	Year	Opening balance	Regular investment each year	End value after 8% net growth	Child one fees – Asha	Child two fees – James	End balance
1	2005	0	4,883	5,051			5,051
2	2006	5,051	5,127	10,757			10,757
3	2007	10,757	5,383	17,182			17,182
4	2008	17,182	5,652	24,396			24,396
5	2009	24,396	5,935	32,477			32,477
6	2010	32,477	6,232	41,507			41,507
7	2011	41,507	6,543	51,578			51,578
8	2012	51,578	6,870	62,789			62,789
9	2013	62,789	7,214	75,247			75,247
10	2014	75,247	7,574	89,069			89,069
11	2015	89,069	7,953	104,382			104,382
12	2016	104,382	8,351	121,325			121,325
13	2107	121,325	8,768	140,048			140,048
14	2018	140,048	9,207	160,714	Asha – 29,371		131,343
15	2019	131,343	0	141,791	Asha – 30,252		111,540
16	2020	111,540	0	120,413	Asha – 31,160	James – 31,160	58,094
17	2021	58,094	0	62,715		James – 32,094	30,621
18	2022	30,621	0	33,057		James – 33,057	0
19	2023	0	0	0			0
Total			95,692		90,783	96,311	

Diagram 5.7: Table showing the planning of schools fees, assuming 8 per cent growth each year, using a spreadsheet programme to calculate required regular investment over 14 years.

In summary

Managed funds are an ideal way to achieve greater growth from your regular savings by blending shares with cash and bonds. Crucially, you reduce your risk compared to direct investment in shares by diversifying across a range of assets and by allowing the professionals to make investments on your behalf.

As we've said throughout, though, there are still risks with these vehicles and it's important that you allocate money to managed funds only as part of a medium- to long-term strategy. As a guideline:

● Try and choose a mix of funds, rather than just one.
● If you're buying through a fixed-term savings plan,

understand the terms and conditions, especially the consequences of stopping or cashing in before your savings term is completed.

- Be prepared for ups and downs in the fund value.
- Remember that volatility can actually work to your advantage, if time is on your side.
- Be prepared to wait for the growth to come through!

In the next part of the book, we'll study the basics of stocks and shares, and learn how to invest safely and wisely in the stock market.

But before we do, there's one final savings project we need to look at. It's likely to be the biggest single cost of your life, so the sooner you get started, the better.

Chapter six

Retirement planning

If you asked the man in the street what the single biggest cost in his life was likely to be, he would probably say his house. Someone else might say their car. A third might sigh and say their partner!

In reality, they are all wrong. The single biggest cost in your life is going to be planning for your retirement.

We've devoted this entire chapter to retirement planning because it is so important in expats' lives. And now more than ever. With the changes in the world's demography, social fabric and work patterns, it is inevitable that long-term saving will become more and more crucial if you are going to have an enjoyable lifestyle in your later years.

What's more, the nature of long-term saving will also have to change if we are to enjoy this lifestyle. Since we're living longer, we need to structure new ways of providing income for longer periods of time during our older years. This particularly applies to expats, who may be outside the traditional models of state-sponsored saving and for whom greater self-reliance has always been the key. Many of us, for example, may choose to retire outside our country of birth and since paying tax has never been an expat's favourite activity, it is doubly important that we know how to build our own long-term 'social security'.

In this chapter we're going to learn the principles of modern financial planning for the long term. This will help you enjoy a great retirement.

In particular, you will learn how to build your retirement fund, where to invest your monies and how to take your income in retirement so that your family will have something left when you are long gone!

The principles of retirement planning

Retirement planning is, quite simply, long-term saving. But rather than saving for a specific goal, such as a yacht or a deposit for a home, you're saving to provide a future income. You are building replacement income for the time after paid employment ceases. So, you have to build a pot that will sustain you for the rest of your life. And that could be a very long time indeed.

There are two parts to retirement planning. You need to build funds quite aggressively during the 'saving' period, then invest them for income during the 'draw-down' period. If you haven't invested enough during the savings period, you will have a short and rather miserable existence after retiring; alternatively, if you don't invest wisely when the time comes to draw on that money, it could all go rather quickly, again leaving you with nothing!

Remember, we're all living longer than ever before and our life expectancy rises every year. As such, the period during which we take income from our pot could be as long

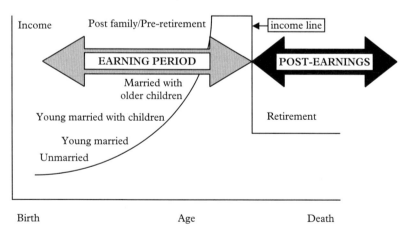

Diagram 6.1: The seven stages of life showing the earnings period versus non-earning period in a typical lifespan. Note the dramatic drop in income after retirement.

as, if not longer than, the period during which we built the fund in the first place. For example, let's say you start saving for your retirement at 27 years of age, and you retire at 55, this means you have been saving for 28 years. And if you live to 93 (not unreasonable for someone now aged 27), your savings during your working life have paid for 38 years without working. That's 38 years of free money!

And who wouldn't want that?

The aim is to raise your post-earnings income line, by modifing your consumption patterns during your earning period. Look at the diagram below.

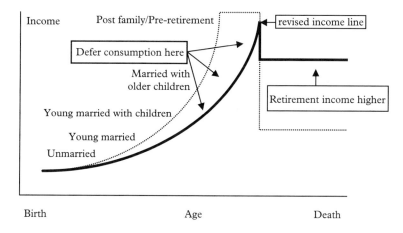

Diagram 6.2: Using the seven stages model to show how to increase retirement income by deferring consumption during earnings period.

You're on your own

But let's get one thing clear right away – the state is not going to provide for you.

Regardless of which country you come from, the pressures on state-run social security programmes are so huge that there will be very little for you when the time comes to retire. In Europe particularly, successive governments were paying money out of pension funds as soon as it came in, feeding the current generation of pensioners with today's contributions rather than investing the money into the retirement fund of the person actually making the contribution. It may sound incredible but, sadly, it's true.

The fact is that state-run social security systems around the world are facing ruin – and governments are urging individuals to take care of their own arrangements.

This is hardly surprising when you consider that today's standard retirement age of 65 was set by Chancellor Otto von Bismarck when Germany established the world's first state pension programme – back in 1898. At that time, the average life expectancy was 45! Nowadays, the life expectancy has almost doubled, but the retirement age has stayed the same.

So, the state is not going to look after you. Even if it were capable of doing so, as an expat, you are out of the system and will be unlikely to benefit anyway.

"But what about the company I work for?" you might ask. This is certainly true back home, where many companies provide company pension schemes. But it is very rare to find this offshore. Quite simply, companies in the Middle East do not have to provide pensions, and consequently they don't.

So it's up to you. You have to build a pot that will provide replacement income for the rest of your life when you leave paid employment. And for those people who say they will never stop working, that's fine – but surely it would nice to have the choice to just stay at home and do nothing some days wouldn't it?

Let's look now at how to build your retirement pot.

Building the pot

As we said at the beginning of this chapter, there are two stages to a successful retirement – building the pot and then drawing from the pot. Now we're going to look at building your pot.

We have talked before about windows of time or 'time horizons'. In planning your pension, your time horizon is that date in the future when you want to have the freedom to pack it all in and sail off into the sunset. Thus, if you're in your early 30s now, and your chosen retirement date is 60, you have just 30 years to build your pot. This is your retirement savings window.

Conversely, if you're already 50 and want to retire at 65, your time horizon is that much closer and the savings window is correspondingly shorter.

The length of this temporal window dictates our pension planning in two ways:

1. Because of the power of time in building money, the earlier you start the better – since your money will have longer to grow.
2. Remembering reward requires risk demands time, the longer your window, the more aggressive you can be.

To examine the first point, let us consider the following two examples.

Mrs Good and Mr Slow both want to retire in the UK on £20,000 a year from age 65. If Mrs Good started her retirement savings when she was 25, she would have to set aside £112.50 per month.[1] Mr Slow, however, waits until he is 35 before thinking about getting a pension plan started and when he does, he is told he will have to contribute £250 a month till he retires – for exactly the same end result. By delaying ten years, he has to pay twice as much!

We can approach this another way. Mrs Good starts her pension planning at 25. Her friend, Mr Slow, starts his at 35. Both contribute a set £200 per month until they retire at 65. Assuming all other factors remain the same, Mrs

---

[1] For the purposes of this example, we have used the following parameters – steady growth of seven per cent a year, contributions increasing by three per cent a year to match inflation of three per cent.

Good can retire with more than double the fund of Mr Slow, roughly £256,000 more! That means she could have an extra £12,800 a year for life.[1]

So, getting started early is a key issue. A useful rule of thumb is as follows:

Years to Retirement	Percentage of Salary to set aside
20	20%
15	33%
10	67%
5	130% – impossible!

So the first step is to establish your time horizon . . . in how many years' time do you wish to retire?

This then raises another question – how long do I want to contribute into my pot for? What if I wanted to retire in 20 years, but would rather get all the funding out of the way in the next five years?

This is particularly relevant for expats. Many of us have a window of accelerated earnings whilst offshore. For example, this could be five years in the Gulf as part of an international career, before returning to our home countries.

This is an ideal time to set the foundations for a very comfortable retirement. Using the principle of time windows and allowing for the compounding power of time, a period of high savings early on in life, during a period offshore, can often yield spectacular results. And it can also be a lot easier for you than trying to save for 20 years back home!

Let us look at an example. Rajan works for an accountancy firm in London, but is seconded to their Saudi office at the age of 26.

He spends five years there before taking up a promotion in New York. During his time in Saudi he is able to

---

[1] Assumes growth of seven per cent a year, no inflation and no contribution increases. Assumes life expectancy of 78 and taking income of five per cent a year from the retirement fund.

comfortably set aside $1,500 per month, into aggressive managed funds.

At the end of this 5-year period of intense saving, Rajan has contributed $90,000 to his 'retirement fund'. By the time of leaving Saudi, it has grown to $110,000. He then leaves the money rolling up in his 'retirement fund', safe in the knowledge that for the rest of his working life he need not contribute another penny to a pension plan. By the time he chooses to retire at the age of 50, his fund has grown to over half a million dollars. [1]

This is good financial planning – making the best use of your time and circumstances to build freedom in the future.

So, now it's just a case of choosing a pension plan and off we go, right?

Planning for retirement . . . not buying a pension

As we have seen above, the length of our retirement savings window will determine the broad structure of where we should put our funds, in terms of risk and reward.

Less time means less risk and thus saving into places like cash, bonds, and guaranteed-return funds. More time allows us the option to take more risk in the search for better returns, so this will mean managed funds, individual holdings of shares or even alternative investments such as derivatives or property.

But surely, you might be thinking, if I want to save for retirement, I just get a pension plan, right? After all, this is going to give me an income in retirement, isn't it?

Well, yes and no.

A useful way to approach your retirement planning is to get rid of the concept 'pension plan' and to simply think about long-term saving or retirement saving. This will allow

---

[1] Assuming his investment fund grows at a steady 9.5 per cent a year. Does not allow for effects of inflation.

you to think more creatively about what you are trying to achieve and how you might go about it. It might also free you up from negative concepts about pensions. One of the reasons people don't like to get into planning their retirement is the negative associations we have with pensions – mis-selling scandals, fear of getting locked into something we can't get out of, resentment of agents' commissions, and the associations with old age (particularly for someone in their 20s!).

But there's another, more simple, reason to forget the term 'pension plan' while we're offshore. Strictly speaking, they are not available to many expats!

Let's explain. A pension plan is a vehicle designed to build an income for another financial vehicle, known as an *annuity*, that starts to pay out once you retire. Both the pension plan and the annuity have specific tax and legal considerations defined by your home country. But, once you are outside the financial system of your home country, you might no longer be eligible to start any financial vehicle there – particularly not one with tax benefits like a pension. You have to be a resident to be eligible.

So, strictly speaking, expats can't really have pension plans like the ones they could have back home.

But this may not be such a loss after all.

In many of our home countries, pension plans are marketed by financial institutions as the vehicle to provide an income later in life. There are specific rules governing pension plans to make them more attractive to savers, encouraging us to save for that far-off date – remember, governments want us to save for our retirement, as we will be less of a burden to the state that way. The main sweetener for many pension plans in our home countries is tax-free growth on the funds. This is quite a benefit, considering that virtually all other savings vehicles are taxed by the state one way or another.

But there is a problem. Home country pensions have two key restrictions. First of all, the rules are usually very tough about what you may and may not do with your money. You're not usually allowed access to your money until a set age and you can face heavy charges (set by the financial institutions offering the pensions plan) if you stop your contributions.

And, secondly, when the time comes to access your funds, you have no choice about how to take your funds. In many European countries, your domestic pension plan must be used to buy an annuity. And this is a very considerable restriction on your freedom.

An annuity is an annual income for life. In simple terms, the financial institution offering the annuity will set your yearly income from your pension fund by comparing your average life expectancy with your accumulated pension fund and simply dividing it up by the number of years you're expected to live. If you live longer than average life expectancy, you win. If you don't, the annuity provider wins.

And there's more. Remember that pensions were supposed to be tax-free? Well, the growth on many domestic pension plans during the savings period is tax-free, but when it is time to take the benefits of all those hard years of saving . . . what the state giveth, the state taketh away. You will have to pay tax on your home country pension as if it were earned income. That could be as much as 40 per cent tax for some people, just when they were hoping to relax and enjoy life! So domestic pensions may not be such a good thing after all.

Being offshore, thankfully, you are outside many of these rules and restrictions. So, forget about 'pension plans' and think instead about long-term saving, or retirement planning. It will be better for your wallet, easier to get started, and much more flexible in the long run.

By the way, if you come across offshore plans described as pension plans, this is simply a marketing term – they are standard savings contracts dressed up to look like pension plans. This is not to criticise those plans – it is useful to have boxes in which to allocate our funds – but strictly speaking they are just standard offshore savings plans.

So, having established our time horizon and committed

67

ourselves to planning for retirement (instead of 'getting a pension'), how do we structure the project? How do we know what we need and what we must contribute to get there?

This is where a good plan comes in.

Drawing up your plan

First of all, you will need to set clear objectives on what is it you want to achieve and what you can do to get there.

This means you must establish how much it is you require each year as an income when you want to retire. Many of us have no idea. Perhaps that's why many of us will live in poverty when we are older. As the saying goes, we may not actually plan to fail, but if you fail to plan. . . .

So, set clear objectives on how much you'll need each year. A useful way to do this is to compare this with your current income. Will you need more or less in retirement? Will your out-goings be higher or lower? Will the house be paid off? Will the children have completed their education and be financially independent (tricky one, this). And what about transport and holidays?

As a useful rule of thumb, most people find that they can live very well in retirement on about two thirds of their earned income level. Assuming that the house has been paid off, the children are independent and there are fewer bills to pay in general, this will ensure a very comfortable standard of life.

The next step is to consider your contribution window. This may be different from your retirement window. As we saw earlier in the example of Rajan, you may decide that your retirement is 20 years away, but you want to get it all sorted out in five. So, you only want to contribute to your retirement fund for five years, and let the fund build up of its own accord for the remaining 15 years. This is particularly suitable for expats who, like Rajan, find themselves with an accelerated window of earning during which they really can set themselves up for life.

Remember, it's the time when we wish to access the money that determines how aggressive we can be, not how long we want to contribute for. In Rajan's example, although he was only contributing money into funds for five years, he could afford to be quite aggressive because it was about 20 years before he might wish to call on that money.

And that's it. Almost. Once you've established your desired income and your contribution/retirement windows, you can then build a spreadsheet to plot what you need to do.

And this is where we learn the fundamental key of modern retirement planning.

The rule of twenty

At the beginning of this chapter, we talked of building your own fund, then drawing from that fund.

When the time comes to start taking your income, the size of your fund will obviously determine how much you can take out. The bigger your fund, the more you can draw down. The more you have to live on.

But two problems remain – if you are planning your retirement now for 30 years in the future, how do you know what fund size to aim for? You might know what income level you need, but how can you relate this to the size of pot you need to build to provide this income? And, linked to this, how can you be confident that your income withdrawals will last for the rest of your life, when you don't know how long this could be?

In other words, how do you calculate the size of your retirement pot, in the hope that it will generate your chosen level of income from your chosen retirement date *and continue to do so until you die*, which could be 30 or 40 years later?

This is where the rule-of-twenty can help. In essence, you should plan to build a pot *20 times the annual income* you need in your time of retirement.

69

So, if you want to be financially independent with an income of $40,000 per year, you'll need to have a pot of $800,000 at your retirement date. Using this formula, you could live on about $40,000 a year in perpetuity. Because the income level is sustainable, it can remain the same for life and, when you die, the same amount is left for your children. You are simply taking off the growth.

Sounds great. But how does this work?

In this example, we've assumed that your investments continue to grow at 10 per cent a year. You are taking 5 per cent income each year ($40,000 out of $800,000) which means that there's another 5 per cent safety cushion to allow for inflation and management charges.

If you did not allow for inflation (say, 3.5 per cent) gradually the purchasing power of either your withdrawals or the money left in the pot will decline. Likewise, if you didn't allow a margin for the charges of running your retirement investments (say, 1.5 per cent), your returns could be a lot lower than you've projected.

So, your pot is growing at 10 per cent a year, you take 5 per cent, inflation eats 3.5 per cent and the company managing your money takes 1.5 per cent. You then know that you can continue to take 5 per cent from your fund every year for life without eroding capital, or reducing the real value of your money – and leave it all behind for your family when you go! This truly is long-term financial planning.

If you do not think that 10 per cent is realistic, consider a growth rate of 8 per cent. If your pot continues growing at 8 per cent and you take out 4 per cent, then that leaves another 4 per cent to allow for inflation and charges.

So, as a rule of thumb, between 4 and 5 per cent withdrawals on money growing between 8 and 10 per cent will allow for sustainable income for the rest of your life without eroding capital.

And the key issue here is 'sustainable'. With many of us living longer and longer, but also wishing to get out of paid employment earlier and earlier, it's crucial that whatever plans we make with our money do not run out after 10 or 15 years. If you're planning to create an income for later in life, ensure you have an income *for life*.

So, now we know how much we need to have in our pot at point of retirement to provide a sustainable income for life.

Your next step is simply to create a funding model that will build this pot. Calculate as follows:

1. When do I want to retire?
2. How long do I wish to put money aside for this project?
3. How much will I need at point of retirement?

Working back with a simple spreadsheet, you can establish how much you'll need to save on a regular basis.

If this means putting away a lot of money, don't be surprised. As we said at the beginning of this chapter, funding your replacement income is likely to be the biggest single cost of your life. But either you do it, or you don't – it's up to you.

So, now we know how much we need to set aside. The next question is, where do we put it all?

Where to invest for retirement?

Having decided to build our own retirement strategy, and having designed the funding model so we can maintain an income for life, we now need to consider where we should direct our savings.

This is relatively simple. All you need do is construct a savings portfolio to suit your own goals and risk profile. Here are some basic principles:

1. Start, as always, with the principle *reward requires risk demands time* – if your time horizon is long (and this means 20 years and more), be aggressive; if it is shorter be correspondingly cautious. As we discussed in the chapters about saving, aggressive vehicles will tend to provide a better return on your money than safe ones, but you'll need time for this return to come through. This time cushion is to ride out any market volatility

71

and, in the case of structured financial products (savings
plans), to outweigh the effects of entry charges. If your
time horizon is short – ie you are already close to
retirement age or you wish to retire early, you should
consider reducing the amount of risk you take with your
funds. This means allocating more of your money to
cash and smooth-return vehicles and correspondingly
less to aggressive share-based funds. Of course, there's
always a place for some high-risk vehicles if you desire,
but these need to be part of a carefully thought-out
portfolio strategy. We'll discuss this more in chapter 10.

2. *Diversify* your funds as much as possible – try and have
a mixture of asset classes and within those classes,
diversify. For example, if you're going to have 70 per
cent of your retirement project in managed funds, have
a mix of funds (according to your risk/return/time
profile) and try different fund managers.

3. *Monitor* your money, but don't be obsessive – as one
financial expert said "looking at your plants too often
can tempt you to pull them up and look at the roots . . .
and looking at the roots isn't very good for plants."[1]
Check once a year, don't be neurotic if you're down in a
particular year, but if a particular investment has tanked
and shows no signs of picking up, ditch it.

4. *Switch out of aggressive* funds when your time horizon
approaches – for example, it would be a good idea to
pull out of high-risk funds after a period of high growth
when you have five years or less to your chosen
retirement date. A market downswing then could really
eat into your retirement funds – or keep you in that day
job for a few more years than you'd hoped!

5. Consider some money in *locked-away contracts* if you have
poor discipline. These are likely to be marketed as offshore
pension plans and will have set penalties (charges) if you
try and access funds before your chosen retirement date or

---

[1] Paul Samuelson, American economist and Nobel Prize winner (1970).

72

have to reduce your contribution level. But be sure you understand the effect of these charges before getting into the contract – and are comfortable with the consequences. And only contribute an amount into these plans that you can sustain if you have to return to your home country – they only deliver good value if you keep to the set payment throughout the contract term.

6. Consider *flexible* managed investments for variable amounts or for any amount you wish to save in addition to a contractual savings plan, described above. For short-term expats, this could be the high disposable income excess you have during a period offshore, which may not be sustainable upon return to home country. Either buy these funds through a plan (make sure it is flexible though) or simply chose your own collection of managed funds from different providers.

7. Consider alternatives to funds or money assets when building a pot for your retirement. An illiquid asset such as *property* can be a good way of diversifying your holdings and building your pension fund, provided of course that you can sell it when the time comes to retire. If you don't need to, of course, a rented property can provide valuable additional income in retirement.

Many of these investment ideas are explored in more detail in the next section of the book. The key issue to remember here is that retirement savings doesn't automatically mean 'pension plan' – it is simply *saving with the long term in mind.* Any sort of saving or investment project can be used to help fund your replacement income when the time comes to stop paid employment.

Retirement case study

Mark is 33, earns the equivalent of $40,000 per year as a quantity surveyor and has a dream of retiring at 50, after which he intends to play golf all day every day for the rest of his life. He is committed to saving as much as he can

while in the Middle East to achieve his goal and has
decided to blend a range of different strategies to get there.

First of all, he has an offshore 'pension plan' into which
he pays $350 each month, which rises by 5 per cent every
year and is set to stop on his 50th birthday. He calls this
his 'foundation plan' and it's the fallback he'll keep going
in the unlikely event that he has to stop everything else. His
provider gives a wide range of funds from a number of
different investment managers and he's chosen 10 quite
aggressive funds. Although there are penalties if he stops
the plan, Mark is comfortable that he could maintain the
savings level if he had to return home.

On top of this, Mark also puts $1200 per month into a
basket of mutual funds, again with 10 different investment
houses managing his money. This is under a flexible
umbrella-type plan that allows him to move between these
different fund managers with some discounts. Because this
plan is completely flexible Mark knows that he can stop
and start at any time. He plans to be in the Gulf for
another seven years, but knows that nothing is ever certain.
All being well, however, he will contribute at least $1200
per month for the remainder of his time offshore.

Mark also invests $200 a month into a mix of shares.
These are quite volatile and fluctuate in value quite
significantly from time to time but he is not discouraged.
As they are part of a long-term strategy, Mark is still
comfortable to invest into them regularly as the long-term
record of the companies is good and they operate across a
range of different areas.

Lastly, Mark owns a house in his native UK. Although
it's heavily mortgaged (with a debt of £75,000 still owing),
Mark has been able to let it constantly since he bought it
three years ago, as a buy-to-let investment. He paid a 15 per
cent deposit, with the remainder being raised through an
offshore bank mortgage. The tenants pay rent on a monthly
basis, which effectively covers Mark's mortgage. The house
has risen in value since his purchase and is now worth

£150,000 but he's chosen to hold onto it until the mortgage is paid, by his 50th birthday. At this point, he will either sell the house, or keep it to provide an additional income.

Taking all of the above into consideration, and assuming a net 10 per cent growth a year, Mark estimates that he'll be able to stop paid employment at age 50 and enjoy a replacement income for life of around $40,000 per year. Given that his current income is $40,000 and that he may live for up to 40 years after 'retiring' on an income that will never be depleted, he is pleased with his disciplined planning. His family should be pleased too – when he dies, his total accumulated funds, worth well over half a million dollars, will pass to his wife and children.[1]

However, he does need to remember that $40,000 by the time he reaches 50 may not be able to buy quite what it can buy today, because of inflation. Assuming inflation stays at 2.5 per cent, his income for life would likely be more equivalent to today's $27,000. This is closer to the two thirds of current income that most people feel they could live on in retirement.

Mark has also protected all of his clever planning by laying his foundations first of all: he has life and critical illness insurance, his company provides medical cover and he is about to take out an income-replacement plan to cover him until he reaches 50. He is pretty determined to reach his goal!

---

[1] Nearer the time, Mark will also take professional advice on any inheritance tax consequences of leaving such a large sum to his dependents.

Section three

Investing
accumulated capital

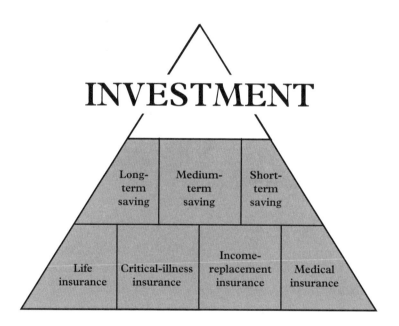

Chapter seven

Investing for beginners – the stock market

Now you're at the top of the pyramid!

You have learnt about laying your foundations. You've chosen insurance packages that are relevant to you. You've seen the benefits of deferring consumption and are allocating your current disposable income into savings boxes for short-, medium- and long-term needs. You also have a clear plan on how you're going to fund your retirement.

So, having done all of that (assuming you have any money left!), it's time to look at investing.

Investing, for us, is a lump-sum activity. It is different from saving, which is primarily concerned with building funds for the future. When you're saving, the returns on your money tend to be an added bonus. When investing, these returns are the whole point. We invest to make more money.

The remainder of this book will give you a basic introduction to investment. While we can't pretend to cover everything, the following four chapters should provide you with a solid grounding on the basics and give clear guidance on how to invest lump sums successfully – whether you choose to buy shares directly, or invest in packaged products. We'll start with the stock market.

Stocks and shares

Most investment activity around the world is connected one way or another with stocks and shares. So, this is a good place to start our exploration of basic investment principles.

A stock, or as we prefer to say a *share*, is your very own

holding in a company's fortunes. When you own a share, you literally own a part of the company and thus you *share* in their success.

You don't even have to work at that company to share in their fortunes. Being a shareholder in a company means that you could work somewhere totally unconnected with what they do, yet still benefit from owing part of their business. For example, if you held some shares in Coca-Cola, then you would be one of Coke's owners. Imagine telling that to your friends!

The premise behind this is simple – if the company does well, then you can benefit from your investment in them. You can make money as they make money. On the other hand, if the company doesn't do well, then you don't benefit.

But how does this work?

Since you own part of the company, shareholders are entitled to a *share* of the company profits. If the company has a good year, then the board of directors will distribute the profits to the company's owners – and that means you, the shareholders. These distributions are known as *dividends*, being profits *divided* by shares.

So, you get money simply by owning a bit of a good company – you don't even have to work there or lift your finger at all! Great!

But what if, one year, the company didn't make any profit? Or it actually made a loss? What would happen then?

Well, certainly there would not be any profits to distribute, so you get nothing back from your financial stake in the company. Sure, you still own part of Coke, but it hasn't given you much. You might not feel so good about that. And other people might feel the same and consider selling their shares in Coke and buying shares in a company that will give them a better return on their investment.

This buying and selling necessitates the existence of a market – a stock market. This is a place where people can buy and sell shares in companies, which are open to public ownership. Companies such as these are listed on a public market, so they are known as publicly-listed companies.

What drives the prices of different companies' shares on this market is the relative attractiveness of each company's prospects for its shareholders. Using the example above, if Coke did not have a good year and did not pay any return to you for your holding in the company, you might sell and buy into another company. But a lot of other shareholders may also be feeling the same way, and not many people would be willing to buy our shares in Coke, because the poor results from last year are public knowledge. So, the price you get for your shares in Coke might be less than if they were in a company that was producing healthy profits.

That is to say, the price of shares in these companies will fluctuate according to how well each company performs each year. Or, more accurately, how well people *think* they are going to perform.

This is a key point. Rather than waiting for a company to do well, and having to compete with lots of other people to buy their shares (and pay inflated prices in the process because demand may outstrip supply), the smart investor may choose to buy his shares *before* the company announces its profits. In other words, he or she will buy his or her shares when the prices are still reasonable *in the expectation* that the company will do well soon thereafter and that he or she would have paid less than somebody who buys the shares a few months later.

Thus, it is the *expectation* of good results, or the earnings that you can make on your share purchase, that drives share prices.

In this example, if that same smart investor chose to sell his shares a few months later, after the good results have been declared and everybody wants a piece of that company, it is most likely that he can sell them for more than he paid. In just a few months, he has made a profit. Just by sitting in his chair and choosing which companies to invest in. . . .

This *buying and selling on future expectations* is the basic principle behind stock-market investing.

What determines the price of a share?

Most people buy and sell their shares in companies in the hope that the company will do well, or announce some good news that will encourage others to buy that share, and this pushes up the prices. Some hold the shares for a long time, others for much shorter.

Long-term investors will hold shares in a company for their annual dividends (the share of profits). They will also be pleased if, during the period of their ownership, the value of those shares rises and they can sell their shares at a profit, perhaps some 10 or 20 years later.

Short-term investors may prefer to get in and out for a quick profit, relying on company news to drive up their holdings. They will be less interested in dividends – what they want is for the share prices to go up quickly.

In both instances, it is the expectation of future earnings that drives the price of a share. Good news, such as a well-received new product, or a take-over of a competitor, will ultimately translate into better profits. And better profits will mean greater dividends for the owners – you and the other shareholders.

So, the most fundamental driver of share prices is that company's prospects. If observers think the company is set to do well, the price of the share will rise. If something happens to damage this confidence, then people sell, it's harder to find buyers, and thus the price of each share tends to go down.

Blue-chips versus high-risk companies

Some companies are very solid and long-term performers. Perhaps they've been around for along time, or they dominate a particular market segment. These companies tend to provide solid reliable profits most years and they thus provide good steady returns to those people who own shares in them.

Because these companies are top quality, they're often likened to diamonds. The best type of diamond is known as a blue-chip diamond, hence these companies are known as blue-chip companies and their shares as blue-chip shares. In the relative world of shares, these are generally lower-risk investments.

At the other end of the risk spectrum, there are plenty of other businesses that are less well established. Perhaps they have a smaller market share, their product might be new or experimental, or their management team might be subject to frequent changes.

A typical example of this type of company is a bio-technology firm that researches and develops new medicines. Imagine a company that is developing a cure for cancer. They haven't been around long, they don't have much of a management team, they have a poor track record, but they have apparently stumbled across a plant in South America which has so far proved very effective in stopping certain cancers in tests.

If you could invest in this before everyone else hears about it, the returns on your investment could be spectacular. Imagine the sales potential of a cancer cure!

On the other hand, if their wonder drug takes too long to come to market, or fails a government test, or actually proves useless, then your investment could be rather worthless. Nobody is going to want to buy your share in a company that hasn't got a saleable product – so you're unlikely to get a good price when you want to sell your holding.

So, the *returns* from your shares are linked to the *risks* you're prepared to take in selecting which company to invest in.

Blue-chip stocks tend to be seen as long term, safe investments because they provide a regular dividend and their share price tends to remain fairly steady. Everybody knows and respects these companies: they tend to do well every year and it is highly unlikely that the company will ever go bust.

More speculative companies provide a bumpier ride. Their share might do nothing for years and then suddenly shoot up, by hundreds of percent, if the company gets it right. The variability of returns is significantly greater. These companies may not even pay a dividend since they don't yet have any profits to share, so the focus on your investment here is the hope of future growth in the share price.

So, each company share will represent a *specific* risk, which is determined by the nature of that company. Steady companies are generally low risk, more speculative companies are higher risk.

However, there's also another risk that affects investing in shares – market risk.

Market risk – when even the best investors get burnt

You may have heard of the S&P 500 or the FTSE 100. These are stock-market indices.

An index is the composite value of the top 100 or top 500 companies traded on that market. For example, the US S&P 500 index comprises the top 500 companies (by size) that are traded on this market. The index tracks the overall aggregate value of the shares of all of these companies and as such tends to reflect the broad trend in buying and selling of a particular market. If a market index rises by 5 per cent, it means that, on average, the share value of each of the companies comprising that index has risen by 5 per cent. If the index falls, then the shares in that index have fallen.

Stock-market indices reflect the value of companies, and companies exist to make profits. When the outlook for making money is good, consumer confidence is high and prices tend to go up. We saw this during the 1990s in the United States of America. Everyone was making money, we thought it would go on forever, and everyone wanted a piece of the action.

Conversely, when something happens in the world that may affect the potential of companies to make money, then individuals tend to get scared. Examples would be conflicts, political instability, even environmental issues – all of which may impede a particular business, or business in general, from making the sort of returns that shareholders want. Many individuals then take their money out of shares, thinking that their returns won't be very good in the future. Often they will sell shares and buy bonds, which give a fixed rate of return, or even put the money in the bank, to earn interest.

Even a totally unconnected event can affect the value of your investment, purely by affecting the confidence of stock-market investors. This confidence, once lost, is often slow to return.

For example, following the attacks in New York in September 2001, global markets dropped almost overnight by as much as 30 per cent. Even shares that had absolutely no connection with the USA, the travel industry, insurance or any other business conceivably affected by the attacks, were hit, and hit hard. Panic had set in.

Even 10 months after the attacks, shares in Europe and Asia were upto 40 per cent down from their highs before September 2001. So, there is a secondary risk associated with investing in the stock market, independent of whether your purchase was a good one or not. This is the risk that external, unrelated events could affect business confidence and cause a selling frenzy. Because this risk is generic, and not associated to your individual stock picking, it is known as market risk or *systematic* risk.

This systematic risk is made worse by the very openness of the markets. Because the buying and selling happens publicly, on a market whose *every transaction* is tracked, analysed and commented upon, it is all too easy for a bout of selling to spark panic. And panic is infectious. Stock markets are the reflection of our collective greed and our collective fear. As much as they tend to over-react on the way up, they also overshoot on the way down. *Choosing a great share cannot always protect you from this.*

Now that we have established the two main risks affecting share investing, let's consider how some people make money from the markets.

Buy and hold

The majority of smart investors will buy shares to hold for the long run. They accept that there will be ups and downs in the value of their shares. The ups will be caused by good company news, the downs will be caused by bad news. And, once in a while, a totally unexpected event will blow their share values right out of the water.

But, if it is a good company, they'll come back.

Research by the investment company Templeton showed that a long-term view is essential to successful investing.

Between 1954 and 1996, they found that markets going in an upward direction tended to last an average of four years, whereas down markets lasted one year. Respectively, these are known as bull and bear markets.

On average, the total appreciation during a bull market has been in the region of 100 per cent (allowing for inflation), and the average bear market decline 25%. Each bear market has been succeeded by a bull market even more rewarding than the one before it.

So, bull markets and bear markets will always be with us. There will always be a time when investor sentiment is positive, and there will always be times when it's negative. Whilst a bear market is unpleasant, though, it is an integral part of investing.

But what if we wanted to try and time the market?

86

What if we thought we could predict when stocks were going to go up and when they were going to go down? Wouldn't we make a lot of money doing this?

A question of timing

The very success of making money on your chosen asset relies on it growing in value from the point at which you bought it. If you're investing in any asset whose value goes up and down, then there will be times when it's better to purchase and times when it's not such a good idea.

If you buy an asset when its price is relatively high, then the chances that it may drop in value afterwards are much higher than if you had bought when the price was low. Buying low and selling high is the commonly recited mantra.

Ironically, most people tend to do the exact opposite. Because we follow the herd, because we listen to the 'expert' on the television, because we are rarely brave enough to make our own contrary decision, most of us tend to buy at the top of a market and sell at the bottom.

Following the herd is the most common reason for buying at the wrong time. We see our friends making money and we want some of that, so we buy what they have. But we often buy *after* the growth has happened, and where the only direction is down!

And then we compound our problems by selling out just at the bottom! We think the share is rubbish, that we have been duped, that the stock market is a con, so we get out of the whole thing, thereby realising a substantial loss.

Because of our *emotional* response to investing, we tend to buy and sell at precisely the wrong moments.

In fact, there *is* a time to buy and a time to get out. As anyone will tell you, try to buy when prices are low, when the investment may in fact appear unattractive to others for example, and then wait for it to grow. Sell when you have made your money. Don't be greedy – don't wait for it to reach 'the top', since you will never know in advance when this is – simply sell when you have made your money and look elsewhere.

And, as a general rule, when everyone around you starts saying a particular share or investment is a sure thing, and your taxi driver starts giving you stock tips, get out!

In broad terms, then, we think there are good times to get into investments and good times to get out. Hopefully, by following this general sentiment, you will avoid the routine drubbings inflicted on most of the investing public.

However, that is not to say that we advocate a constant chopping and changing of your investments. This sort of behaviour is not good for your investments.

Do not confuse *investing* with *trading*. Investing is about choosing a good asset at a good time and holding it for a good period of time. Trading, by contrast, is trying to make a quick buck by getting in and out of the market.

Trading by amateurs, and particularly the day-trading phenomenon common in the late 1990s, may be an exciting way to avoid doing whatever you're employed to do in the office – but it is rarely profitable. You cannot realistically expect to time the market and win more than half the time (in which case the exercise is, statistically, pointless). And you'll waste a lot of energy, time and additional money in trying to do so.

Research performed by Fidelity Investments (see diagram 7.1 on opposite page) showed that people who attempt to time the market often end up losing more money than if they had remained invested. If you were in an asset and kept on jumping in and out, missing just a few days of each year can seriously reduce the overall returns of your portfolio.

This was made even clearer by research conducted by two professors at the University of Calfornia in the US, between 1991 and 1996. Studying 60,000 households which held share-trading accounts, they found that those who traded the most achieved a 10 per cent a year average return, compared to the market's average return

Average Annual Returns (%)		
Index	UK All Share	USA S&P 500
Stay fully invested	14.8	16.6
Best 10 days missed	10.7	12.5
Best 20 days missed	8.8	9.7
Best 30 days missed	6.8	7.5
Best 40 days missed	5.2	5.3

Diagram 7.1: Source – Fidelity Investments annualised returns, MSCI Indices in local currency, net income reinvested to 31 December 1997.

of 17 per cent a year. So, by spending a lot of time and energy trying to beat the market, they ended up underperforming by a massive 59 per cent each year!

The moral is simple: you cannot time the market, just as you cannot predict the future. The best you can do is to make informed judgements about your investment. Try and choose well according to the risk you are prepared to take and according to the time horizon you have allocated for that investment.

The basic principle holds true – the greater the return you want, the higher the risk you will have to take, and the longer you may have to wait for this return to come through.

Some tips

If you are going to invest in shares, and we haven't put you off, then here are some basic guidelines to follow:
1. Choose well, according to your emotional risk profile (your behavioural response to drops in value) and your time horizon.
2. Buy shares in companies that you want to invest in and that you understand.

3. Invest at the right time – try not to buy when everybody else is buying or the market is in a frenzy.
4. Avoid 'sure things' – when your taxi driver starts giving you share tips, get out (of the market!).
5. Diversify – it's much riskier to hold one share than it is to hold 10 or 12.
6. Buy more in the troughs – if you have confidence in a particular investment, buy more of it when prices drop.
7. Understand the different risk profiles of different company shares and allow for systematic risk.
8. Don't become obsessive, paranoid, greedy or boastful; shares are meant to increase your wealth, which is supposed to increase your overall happiness – if you can't find any joy through your investing, stop it!
9. Make sure that the rest of your financial plan is in place before you allocate money to shares.

How to buy and sell shares

You can buy and sell shares quite easily. Obviously, the place to do this is on a stock market but, since this is restricted to investment professionals, most of us employ brokers to buy and sell on our behalf.

A broker is someone who will execute your instructions for buying and selling on a public market. He or she will take a charge for this, which was traditionally a percentage of the share price. In more recent years, discount-type brokerage houses have offered to buy and sell shares for a fixed fee, such as $20 per trade.

If you know which company's share you want to buy, or you like to do your own research and selection, you should look for an *execution-only broker*. Many banks offer this service, as well as Internet sites and other financial institutions. They will take your instructions and execute your order at the best possible price, but they won't give you any advice on what you should be doing. That part is up to you.

If you want advice, on the other hand, you will have to pay for it. You will also have to deposit a much larger amount with your broker before he or she will buy and sell on your behalf. In general terms, the entry level to have a full-service stockbroker managing your portfolio could be anywhere between $100,000 and $500,000.

Growth without risk?

For many of us, we would like to make investments that have the growth potential of shares but without the associated risks. Buying and selling shares through a stock market is not for everyone and bad experiences are, sadly, still common.

Likewise, not everyone has $100,000 to invest to engage the services of a private stockbroker.

In recent years, a large number of new products have been developed to cater for the growing market of international investors. The most popular of these products blend the investor's appetite for growth with a more carefully defined risk profile. And since many of these products have low entry levels, they are more accessible to the average man or woman with a bit of money to invest.

Low entry levels, stock market-type growth and lower levels of risk? Sounds very attractive. In the following chapter, we will find out what these products are, how they work and which ones might be suitable for you.

Chapter eight

Lump sum investment products

Investing, as we saw in the previous chapter, is not without its risks.

Whilst shares can offer the potential for great returns, two risks will always remain – specific risk and systematic risk. The first is the risk that the company you choose to invest in does not do as well as expected. The second is the risk that a totally unconnected event could still drive down the value of your share-holdings.

One of the best ways of meeting these risks, and yet still being invested in the market, is to diversify. Rather than holding the shares of just one company, you might hold a range of different companies. This way, if one company does badly, then at least your entire portfolio is not lost.

If you're able to choose companies in different sectors, then you spread your risk further. Rather than putting all your savings into the shares of manufacturing industries, for example, you might also have shares in foodstuffs, fashion, insurance or utilities companies. This means that, should there be a slow-down in one industry, your other shares may not be affected.

You might also choose to invest across a range of different countries, thereby avoiding geographical risk. By having some European shares and Asian or emerging market company shares as well as your home country ones, you again spread the risk of being hit by one specific event, or loss of confidence, confined to your country.

In all of these steps, you are trying to mitigate the

possibility that specific risk and systematic risk wipe out your portfolio.

This is all very well of course, but would only apply if you wanted to take an active role in the management of your investments. Not everybody does. For many of us, having to do all this research and then buying and selling could be quite daunting, even if we had the time and inclination to do so.

This is the key advantage of managed funds or packaged investment products – you pay the professionals to manage your money for you.

Managed funds as lump-sum investments

As we saw in chapter five, managed funds offer a number of key benefits. Your money is being looked after by a professional fund manager who's qualified to make

Look Mum, Dad's made some money on his investments. . . .

94

investment decisions on your behalf. These fund managers have access to a lot of information and the tools to enable them to buy and sell shares quickly. And by spreading your money across a wide mix of shares, bonds and cash, they can minimise the risks of being too heavily invested in one company or one sector.

You also benefit from the pooling effects of a large fund of money. For relatively small investments into a managed fund, your money can be invested in assets that may not otherwise have been accessible to you as an individual investor.

Managed funds are, all in all, a good deal. They are the quickest and simplest way of harnessing growth in the stock markets and offer many benefits over direct shareholdings.

Expats often buy managed funds as lump sum investments through vehicles known as *offshore bonds*. These offer a number of advantages compared to buying funds directly, as we shall see below, and are a popular way to build a personalised investment portfolio.

Offshore bonds

An offshore bond is a packaged product offered by an insurance or 'life' company, such as Royal Skandia or Clerical Medical International. The bond acts as a wrapper around your chosen assets, typically a selection of managed funds.

It is the funds, as ever, that provide the growth on your investment, not the bond. In itself, the bond produces nothing – it's merely a convenient way of packaging your investments. But by wrapping your choice of managed funds in a bond, investors can achieve a number of benefits.

Firstly, all your managed funds are administered through one vehicle. Even if you have 10 different funds under the wrapper of the offshore bond, it is the role of the life company to provide you with all the relevant valuations and updates, usually in one simplified summary format. Having just one point of contact, rather than 10, can be a real benefit.

Each life company bond is likely to offer you a wide choice of funds. For investors unable to perform their own research, or unwilling to do their own buying and selling direct from the fund provider, a offshore bond provides a convenient place to choose a fund or combination of funds that suit.

For those investors who like to buy in and out of funds on a regular basis, the offshore bond can also offer discounts on the costs involved. As each individual fund will tend to have an up-front charge, that has to be paid every time you buy into the fund, regular 'trading' between funds can become expensive. An offshore bond provider, by contrast, will tend to have negotiated entry discounts with the fund managers accessible through the wrapper, which means that you could get into the funds at significantly lower cost.

As a final benefit, offshore bonds offer some element of confidentiality and investor protection. They are mainly regulated in offshore financial centres whose governments enforce strict investor protection laws and where information cannot be routinely divulged to third parties without your express consent.

Nothing, however, is given for free. As you would expect, there is a price to pay for all this. Offshore bonds can be expensive, with initial charges for the wrapper upto 5 per cent of the sum invested.

This is at the top end of what you would expect to pay to get into a managed fund directly, so if you are considering using offshore bonds as a wrapper, be sure that there would be no further charges to enter the underlying funds. Most companies offering these funds run special offers from time to time, so it always worth asking about these – failing which, if you are buying through an intermediary, try asking him or her to get you a discount.

The problem of timing

So, using a wrapper through which to buy your managed funds can bring some benefits. But even if you are buying a number of funds and have wrapped them in a discounted offshore bond, one big problem remains. It applies to any share-based investing, whether you are buying direct or through managed funds. The problem is timing.

As we saw in earlier chapters, the key to successful investment is to buy into something when prices are low and sell out when prices are high. The difference between the two is your gain.

The problem, of course, is knowing when to buy and when to sell.

When you're putting money into the markets as part of a *regular* savings strategy, you mitigate this risk by dollar-cost averaging. Sometimes the prices are higher, sometimes lower, but over time they will rise and you will have benefited from any drops in the market by averaging down.

But it is a different story when you are looking to make lump-sum investments. If you have a sum of $10,000 to invest, for example, then your approach needs to be totally different from saving $80 per month for 10 years. The risk is much greater, because of timing.

If the market falls the day after your investment is made, you have suffered a loss and you may not have another $10,000 to invest – maybe that was all you could afford to invest.

You will then have to wait for the market to rise again before you can even begin to see a profit – and this could take a considerable amount of time. As we saw in chapter five, market falls are measured in days and weeks, but gains tend to be measured in years.

What is more, after a fall, the corresponding gain necessary to return you to your starting point is not the percentage amount you have just dropped – it is higher. For example, if you invest $10,000 and the market drops by 15 per cent the next week, then in order to return to your original investment, you will need a growth not of 15 but 17.62 per cent.

If your $10,000 investment drops by 40 per cent, then gaining 40 per cent again will only take you up to $8,400 – you're still $1,600 short!

In fact you'll need 66.67 per cent growth to take you back to your starting position. And, while 40 per cent drops happen (the US S&P 500 dropped more than 40 per cent between March 2000 and July 2002), it can take a long time for a market to rise 66 per cent!

So a key issue for lump-sum investment is timing. But what can you do to mitigate this risk?

One solution could be to treat every lump-sum investment as a regular investment and drip-feed it into the market. Thus, instead of investing $10,000 all at once, you may choose to invest $833 per month for a year, and thus average-out the price at which you enter the market.

However, this may not be suitable for everyone – particularly if you don't have the time or inclination to keep buying into an investment every month. And there's always the risk that your investments could still go wrong, i.e. that markets could drop after you've done all your carefully phased buying.

So, a key question remains. Are there any investment products that can mitigate these two risks, the first being the risk that your chosen investment drops soon after you have bought in, the second being the more general risk that markets can drop unquantifiable amounts at unforeseen moments?

Or, put another way, are there any investments that will always go up, and never down, in value? And are there any investment products where you can participate in general market gains but can limit any potential downside?

Yes, there are.

Let's look at them.

Packaged profits

Investors, being human, tend to make choices based on fear and greed. If you're starting from a relatively low base, you take greater risks. Conversely, once you have money, you are loath to lose it. When considering a lump-sum investment, which de facto means that you have accumulated some money, the fear of losing it is strong indeed.

This has not been ignored by the investment industry. Packaged products offering secure investment growth are big business. In the next few pages, we look at the two most popular types.

The premise underlying these products is a simple one. You can have the gain, but none of the pain. Or at least, we should note, you can have *some* of the gain: as we shall see, returns from these products will always be less than direct investment in their underlying assets. For many risk-averse investors, though, that's a price they're willing to pay for the peace of mind these products can offer.

With-profits funds

With-profits funds are a peculiarly British invention, rather like warm beer or the game of cricket. They are also big business, with an estimated $500 billion invested this way.

The principle of a with-profits fund is simple – you give the investment company your money to manage, and the end of the agreed investment period you get the money back *with profits*.

With-profits funds became popular because they allowed individual investors to benefit from the growth of financial markets, but without the risks. The fund managers would invest across a wide range of assets and provide regular growth on the policyholders' funds by *smoothing* the returns. If they had a good year, they'd apply some of the growth to the policyholders' funds but keep a portion in reserve. Then if a bad year came along,

99

these reserves could be called up and added to the funds. The result was a smoothing of investment returns – a regular and steady growth instead of volatile swings.

Growth is added to with-profits funds in the form of bonuses. There are two types of bonus: reversionary and terminal. *Reversionary* bonuses are declared each year, and added at the end of the year. *Terminal* bonuses are added at the end of the policyholder's saving period, i.e. when the funds are withdrawn.

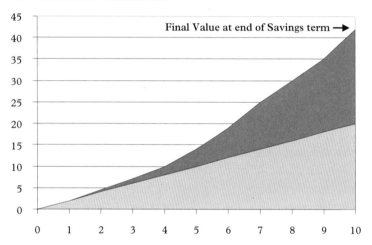

Diagram 8.1: Theoretical example showing increase in value of a with-profits bond due to terminal bonus over time. Terminal bonus is represented by ■ and reversionary bonus by □ .

Much of the overall return from your with-profits investment is contained in the terminal bonus. The longer you can hold your investment, the bigger the terminal bonus is likely to be. In a 25-year with-profits policy, for example, the terminal bonus can amount to as much as two thirds of the overall return. Consequently, these funds tend to favour longer-term investors.

One of the criticisms often levelled at these types of investment is that it can be difficult to know what your fund is worth at any given moment, and what it's going to be worth at the time of withdrawal. The best that the providing company can do, until the actual day comes when you want withdraw your money, is to offer estimates.

The providing with-profits company can also impose penalties on withdrawals in difficult market circumstances, which can sometimes be quite severe. Thus, you sacrifice an element of control in return for the promise of smooth and secure returns.

On the whole, through, with-profits investments are a good long-term lump-sum investment, albeit not very transparent. They can be ideal for lump-sum investors who want a steady growth, and for whom the volatility of funds or direct shareholdings may not be appropriate.

We think that they work best as the foundation, or core holding, of a diversified investment portfolio.

But they are not the only investment in the marketplace catering for the low-risk investor seeking guarantees and protection of capital.

With the continuing uncertainty in global stock markets in the early 2000s, guaranteed investment products have become very popular, targeting first-time investors or anyone else concerned about the security of their capital. Many of these products are offered through banks, whose deposit customers represent an accessible and captive client base.

With low-entry requirements, perhaps as low as $5,000, and the lure of guarantees in uncertain times, these products are very big business indeed.

Like with-profits funds, their attractiveness lies in the promise of growth without risk. However, the underlying structure of these guaranteed products is quite different from the relatively simple concept of smoothed investment returns that drive with-profits funds. As a matter of fact, their underlying structure can often be very complex.

Let us see how they work, and which type may be the most suitable for you.

Guaranteed investments

These are two main types of guaranteed investment. The first is a term-based investment, where you agree to leave your lump sum invested for a set period of time and where the final return is linked to the performance of one or more major stock markets during that period. Your original invested capital is usually guaranteed to be returned. The second type has no fixed time-scale but rather allows you to participate in the on-going gains of the market whilst also limiting your down-side risk.

Put another way, the first type of product offers defined returns, the second offers defined risk.

Fixed-term guaranteed products – defined returns

The typical fixed-term product offers a complete capital guarantee. It will usually offer a minimum return of all your money back at the end of a specified period.

In addition, your money will be linked to the performance of one or more stock-market indices. You will be rewarded with either a bonus if these markets do not fall, or a portion of the growth if they rise in value over the chosen period. Thus, you are guaranteed your original investment to be returned and you get growth depending on what happens in the stock markets.

As markets tend to go up over time, this should be a winning combination. As we saw in chapter five, the markets tend to go up by 100 per cent then drop by 25 per cent: on average, they go up for four years, then down for one. Where people lose money it's because they invest in the wrong asset, at the wrong time, then exit at the wrong time – usually by getting in at the top of a market and getting out at the bottom. With a fixed-term guaranteed product, you're at least protected from making this mistake.

In the worst case with these products, the markets do

not grow as expected during the set period and you just get your money back. Whilst you may have lost an opportunity, you haven't actually lost any money. But be sure that you can afford to keep your money locked away for all this time – if you need to cash-in mid-term, you may crystallise a loss.

On the other hand, when the product succeeds and you withdraw at the end of the set term, you are guaranteed full return of capital plus your bonus dependent upon market performance.

On-going guaranteed products – defined risk

The second type of guaranteed product operates differently. Rather than setting a defined return, they allow the investor to set a defined risk. You participate in the growth of the market, on an on-going basis, but you have set a 'floor', below which your investment may not drop.

You define how much of your investment is used to participate in the market and how much is kept 'capital secure'. The capital secure amount is generally anything between 95 per cent and 99 per cent of your investment – the remainder being used to generate your return.

If the market rises, a bonus is added to your investment. If not, no growth is added, and you have forfeited the amount used to participate in the market. For example, if you wish to be 98 per cent secure and wish to link your investment to the European stock market, a typical fund will use the 2 per cent 'risk capital' to buy a financial instrument that pays out if the market rises over the set term. If the market does rise and you're 'in the money' you either get a pre-defined bonus, or you benefit from a percentage of the market rise. If not, your 2 per cent is forfeited, and your investment now stands at 98 per cent of the original amount.

These products appeal to the investor who wants to know the maximum he could lose at any time. They also

103

appeal to the active investor who wants to get in and out of markets on a regular basic, to benefit from their growth, but who prefers to set a cap on his potential losses.

Guaranteed products – what to look for

Many of these funds look very attractive. Some actually work quite well. However, as with anything in the financial services world, it is worth comparing products to find which offers the best terms and to be sure that yours is suitable for you. And read the small print!

We suggest the following guidelines:

1. As much as possible, try to understand the worst-possible case scenario affecting your fund.
2. Ask yourself how secure is the provider: what comeback do you have if they fail, or one of the companies offering the security fails?
3. Can you get in and out quickly? What are the exit penalties?
4. Does the investment term really suit you?
5. How do the charges impact upon the potential return?
6. If you are being promised income, is this really income or just a withdrawal of your own money?

Some of these products use very clever marketing ploys to make them appear more attractive. You need to be wise to these tricks. Here are some tips:

Look closely at the use of the word *guaranteed*. Check for any asterisks or small print. A guaranteed return of 10 per cent (no strings attached) is different from a guaranteed return of 10 per cent*. Nobody, and that means *nobody*, can offer a guaranteed return of 10 per cent forever, by the way, so be very wary of any product that tells you it can.

Understand that a lot of the marketing literature of

---

*Assuming that neither the S&P, the FTSE nor the Eurostoxx indices go down, up, sideways or move in any way at all, ever, etc. etc.

these funds will use simulated or '*pro-forma*' performance instead of real historical performance. This is a clever trick. Pro-forma performance shows how the fund *might have* performed over the last five or 10 years, for example, if it had been available then. This is because the fund may be new and there is no historical data on how it has performed to date. There is nothing illegal about using pro-forma performance, but you need to check that the figures shown relate to the fund they are promoting. It is not unknown for fund marketers to use simulations whose underlying assumptions have very little relation to the fund they are supposed to advertise.

Understand also, that the guarantee has to be *paid for* somewhere. These funds will always return less than a similar fund without a guarantee. If you want safety, you have to be prepared to pay for it.

Finally, it is essential to read the prospectus of these funds – yes, this means the small print – and try to understand what you are investing in. Sometimes, this can be quite different from the picture painted by the brochure.

On the whole, many of these funds offer a very secure way of getting a better return than cash. Just check that your guaranteed investment product is one of the better ones.

Summary

As we said at the beginning of this chapter, investing is not without its risks. Even with supposed low-risk products, as we have seen above, the old rule of *caveat emptor* still applies.

There are many good low risk-products and you can do well out of them. Used as the foundation of a diversified portfolio, with-profits and guaranteed products provide a solid, if unspectacular, starting point.

But that is all they really are – a starting point. If you're serious about investment, and you want to make real money, you'll have to take on higher levels of risks,

105

knowing that with risk comes reward.

But risk doesn't necessarily mean stupidity. The market does not reward stupidity.

If you are interested in more advanced investing, you will need to know how to take *intelligent* risks. This is where you can really learn from the experts. In chapter 10, we look at the research of two Nobel Prize winners, and how you can use their lifetimes of experience to building a winning portfolio.

But, before that, we take a short diversion away from stocks and shares to visit the world of bricks and mortar.

Chapter nine

Property investment

Making money from property

All round the world, property remains a favourite way of building and keeping wealth. In fact, far more people have their money tied up in houses than in stocks and shares, making property the world's biggest asset class.

Most expats will have a property of one sort or another – for some it's a family home, for others, an investment.

Property can be a great investment. On the whole, it's a relatively safe way to invest and it offers the added *emotional* security of a place you can return to when your time offshore is up, or when you are simply fed up!

Buying property as an investment is also a very useful alternative to financial investments, such as shares, mutual funds or the packaged investments discussed in the previous chapter.

As a part of a portfolio, property diversifies the risk away from purely financial assets and offers the investor the opportunity to participate in a totally different area of growth.

Done well, investing in property can be very rewarding financially. This is the key attraction. A well-thought-out property investment can provide a spectacular rate of return, for a relatively low initial investment.

However, it's also quite easy to make mistakes in this type of investing. In the next few pages we'll look at how property investments work and what can be done to ensure you're one of the successful investors.

What drives property prices?

Just like shares, property prices are driven by fundamental factors. Hype and speculation play a part, albeit less so than in the stock markets, but property prices are shaped primarily by a number of simple and easily identifiable factors.

In earlier chapters we saw how, in the stock market, it's the expectation of future revenues that shape the market's attitude towards a company's shares. If expectations are positive for a particular share, more people will want to buy it, enabling current sellers to command a premium. This drives prices upwards.

In the property market, there is a similar story of supply and demand. But the fundamental driving factors are different.

With property, the initial motivating factor is population movement.

The luxury island resort development turned out to be somewhat smaller than many investors had expected.

A house is a place to live in. If plenty of people want to live in a particular location, this creates a pressure on the existing supply. If supply is not quickly increased to meet this demand (and houses take time to build), each existing property carries a premium, so the sellers can demand a higher price from the buyers.

So, it's the net inflow of people that acts as the initial stimulus behind property price rises. Supply then moderates or boosts this momentum.

In London, for example, there's been a long history of net immigration. For as long as records exist, with the exception of the plague years in the mid-14th century, people have been moving into the city. What's more, this trend is likely to continue: research from the UK anticipates the net population inflow to continue at a rate of at least 5 per cent a year for the foreseeable future.

In previous times, the city limits were fluid and thus housing could expand or contract to meet demand. However, in more modern times, government restrictions, local authority planning requirements and local interests have imposed a cap on new development. Because there are significant pressures on land, which has the net effect of restricting supply, the net inflow of people creates a premium in existing properties. As a result, property prices in London will probably maintain their historical upward trend.

However, net inflow and prevailing supply are not the only factors affecting property. What if the prices are simply too expensive? What happens to the property market when no-one can afford to buy?

It's fairly obvious that the market would collapse.

So, in order for a property market to function, houses have to be within the reach of most ordinary purchasers. They have to be affordable.

If a house is affordable, more people will be able to buy it. Affordability in property means the asking price of the house and its associated maintenance costs. It also, crucially, depends upon the prevailing economic climate –

meaning how easy it is to get finance.

In most developed economies, property purchasers take loans to buy houses. If loans didn't exist, very few people would be able to buy houses, as few would have the ready cash to pay for the total asking price. So the introduction of loans and house financing has allowed a greater number of people to get onto the property ladder.

But it's the cost of this finance, how easy it is to get, and the relative mix of loan-to-deposit that really shapes affordability.

Interest rates play an important part here. When interest rates are low, finance is cheap. This means a loan of $100,000 could be repaid quite easily on a monthly basis. But just a small rise in interest rates could mean vastly increased monthly repayments. And this could make homes unaffordable.

Likewise, if lenders will only advance 50 per cent of the property purchase price, meaning consumers have to pay the remaining 50 per cent out of their own savings, this will attract less buyers into the market than a scheme where 80 per cent or 90 per cent of the property value is available as a loan. The less you have to put down as a deposit, the more you can take as a loan. And the more you take as a loan, the easier it is for people to buy their own properties.

So it is the relative influx of people, the supply of suitable properties, and the prevailing affordability that drive property prices.

This gives us a good starting point. Before undertaking any property investment you need to overlay your proposed purchase with the following three questions:
1. Will there be a net inflow of people during the anticipated term of your investment and for the foreseeable period thereafter?
2. Will the current premium on your proposed house be dampened by a host of new developments, flooding the market with oversupply?
3. Will the financial environment (interest rates, availability

of finance, barriers to entry, overall costs) affect affordability for you and future purchasers?

It is worth asking these questions and being rigorous in your answers. Making a poor property investment can be very damaging to your financial health. We're about to discover why.

Illiquidity – the hidden danger

When property goes wrong, it can go very wrong. This is largely because of the time it takes to exit from your investment. A property sale doesn't happen overnight and unless there's a ready supply of buyers, you could be stuck with your house for a very long time.

Liquidity is a financial term meaning how quickly assets can be transferred from one owner to another. Property is an illiquid asset because there isn't one centralised market for buyers and sellers – you have to create a market, with the help of a real estate agent, for each sale.

The danger arises when you want to sell your property. If this is a bad time, and there's a downturn in the property market, a buyer might not be found for months or even years. And all this time you might be paying a loan on the property.

During such a downturn, the value of your property could actually fall to less than the amount you bought it for and upon which the loan was made. This is called negative equity. It hit people in the UK very hard between the late 1980s and the mid-1990s. After a drastic decline in property prices, it took some areas up to seven years for houses to regain the values at which many had been bought, and upon which the loans were being paid.

Anyone wanting to get out during that time had two options. Either to wait a very long time for a buyer to come along or to sell at a vastly reduced price. So, the one specific danger of property investment is its very illiquidity.

This poses particular risks in newly-emerging property

111

markets. If a lot of your overall wealth is tied up in a property and you cannot sell it, then your property is more of a burden than an asset. So, it is vital that any newly-emerging property developments engender an active secondary market, to buy and sell these properties after their initial construction, or you might be stuck for a long time.

You can mitigate this trap by allocating wisely. Don't have all your money in one property or in one area, and don't have all of your wealth tied up exclusively in property. As we have said throughout this book, diversification is vital in preserving your wealth.

Leveraged property investments

Some of the most spectacular returns from property investments occur when you use a mortgage loan to buy the property, then install tenants whose monthly rents will repay your loan. The idea is that, at the end of the mortgage loan, you have a house which has been paid for by someone else. And any gains in the property value in the meantime are an added bonus!

This is known as leveraged or geared property investment since you're using the loan as a lever to *gear* your purchasing power. Here is how it works.

Consider a house selling for $150,000. You put down $15,000 of your own cash for this house. You take a loan for the remaining 90 per cent of the purchase price from a Bank specialising in housing loans. This then *leverages* your $15,000 to $150,000.

Then you install tenants, who pay you a monthly rent. Assuming your monthly rental income covers the loan repayments and maintenance costs, and that this continues throughout the lifetime of the loan, at the end of the loan period you own a $150,000 house. All for a contribution of $15,000!

There are not many investments that could turn $15,000 into $150,000! Even over 20 years, this is a compound return of 12.2 per cent per year. What's more, property tends to appreciate over time. When you come to sell, you could find that the original $150,000 house is now worth $400,000, a compound return of 17.8 per cent per year.

On the whole, this approach works very well. But, as with any investing, it's not without its risks.

The risks of leveraged property investments

Investing in property this way relies upon one key issue, namely the rentability of the property in which you are investing.

You need to be assured of the following:
1. The property can be easily rented out, both now and in the future.
2. The rental income will cover the mortgage loan, now and in the future.
3. Any increases to the interest rate will and can be covered by your rental income.
4. Your rental income also covers any maintenance and repair works.
5. The project does not create a tax liability that will more than cancel-out any potential gain.
6. You are buying property at a price that offers room for capital growth.

When should I buy?

As with the stock market, there's a time to buy property and a time not to buy. Sadly, since many expats are at the bottom of the information chain, they only learn about the attractiveness of a property investment location after hundreds of other people have made their money there and pushed up the prices in the process. So, you can end up buying at precisely the wrong time!

The key is buying a good, rentable property at a good price. So, what are the other factors you might look for

113

when choosing a property, with the hope of seeing an increase in its value? What signs might indicate the potential for growth?

Try and look for at least some of the following:
1. An influx of population.
2. Factors supporting population growth such as businesses relocating to the area.
3. Desirability of lifestyle, access to shops, parks, neighbourhood.
4. Transport links, public and private.
5. Dynamic 'feel' to the community.
6. Access to good schools, catchment area for prestigious educational facilities.
7. New construction activity, evidence of new housing or social projects
8. Government or municipal plans for the area.

If you buy in a place where plenty of other investors have already bought property, you face two dangers. Firstly, the growth potential on your property may be severely diminished – it may have already experienced significant price inflation and you have gotten in at the top. Secondly, if there's a surplus of other property for rent on the market, the tenant has plenty to choose from. In order to gain tenants, you may the have to drop your desired rent. If this drops below the amount that you have to pay to service the loan, you could be making a loss every month.

If interest rates were then to rise, you could really be in trouble. Even a two per cent rise could mean the difference between $668 per month on a $100,000 loan and $786 per month.[1] You can't pass this increase on to the tenant, as he/she already has plenty of other rental properties to choose from, so you end up further subsidising your property investment out of your salaried income.

Before too long, you could be spending a significant amount of money each month to service a loan on an

---

[1] Based on a five per cent and seven per cent interest rate over twenty years.

114

asset which may have depreciated and which shows little sign of regaining lost value. This is *not* good investing!

Some guidelines to help you

If you are considering a leveraged property investment, follow these general guidelines:

1. Be sure that the property can be let easily and there will always be a good supply of tenants.
2. Try to find areas which have not yet experienced their price appreciation, but which have all the ingredients for this: high employment and signs of further growth, facilities for children, proximity to schools etc.
3. Be sure that your rent can cover your mortgage repayments even if the interest rate applying to your mortgage increases substantially.

Summary

Investing in property, as part of a wider portfolio with a long-term view, is a good idea. You can even make excellent short-term gains from leveraged property purchases: if you've chosen well and your property has risen in value, you can sell it, pay off the outstanding loan and pocket a tidy sum in quite a short time.

But you need to do some hard analysis before buying, just as a surveyor would scrutinise the building itself to be sure there are no hidden horrors.

Perhaps you could do your own financial survey. Are your growth assumptions sound? Is your financial plan built on secure foundations? Is there any risk of other properties flooding the market? And if you need to get out in a hurry, where's the emergency exit?

Chapter 10

Being a successful investor

It would be a foolish man, if not a brave one, who buys a brand-new sports car without having learnt to drive first. It would be a similarly foolish man who buys a house without conducting a survey. And it would certainly take a fool to embark upon a new business venture without researching his market or developing his product.

And yet, this is how many of us approach investment.

It's sad, but true. The vast majority of expats make poor investment decisions. As a result, few make any money on their investments and a high proportion will suffer badly. But given a little understanding, time and effort, this could be quite different.

In this chapter, we're going to suggest some simple techniques to help make you a better investor. You won't become an instant expert, but at least you'll know the fundamentals of good investing. And you don't need an MBA or a maths degree to get there.

The starting point

Investing is a big topic. So big, in fact, that magazines, books, and even university courses are devoted to it. And they only cover a fraction of what there is to know. But the key principle is quite simple.

To be a successful investor means making more money on your investments than you lose. You will lose from time to time, for sure, that comes with the territory. But if you can make more than you lose, you're winning. And to do this, you need to learn one fundamental truth: *successful investors will address their risk before considering their growth.*

117

To begin a deeper understanding of investing then, we must start with risk. It's only by understanding risk and learning how to mitigate it that you can arrive at a secure foundation for actually making money.

Risk

Risk is the possibility of unforeseen outcomes. It is the chance that your end result is not what you had expected, such as losing when you had hoped to win. The higher the risk, the more likely that something unforeseen or unplanned will happen. And since very few of us plan to lose, the most drastic risk is loss.

Consider this in terms of your career. A 'risky' career move is one where the outcome turns out differently from what you had expected – you join a 'start-up' company, or you move to another territory to begin a new role in a new department. In either case, the risk of failure could be quite high. Contrast this with a safe career move, where you know in advance what the new role entails, who your colleagues will be, and where your further progress is assured.

Let's return to investments. A risky investment is one where your outcome cannot be easily predicted, that is to say there's a greater probability that it may involve loss. A safe investment, by contrast, is where you can pretty much plan your outcome in advance.

Risk, in investment, is therefore linked with unpredictability of possible outcomes. It is less to do with the absolute outcome of loss, but rather the possibility of loss. Of course, absolute loss does exist – just ask investors in Enron – but this tends to be the worst-case scenario on a variable scale of outcomes.

A high-risk investment will produce outcomes, or returns, that deviate dramatically from the normal or historical return that you might reasonably expect. By contrast, a low-risk investment is one where you are pretty sure of the outcome and all historical evidence supports this expectation.

In the following section, we look at how risk is quantified in the world of investment theory.

When we consider the variability of returns in investment portfolios, this risk is often measured using *standard deviation*. This is the amount by which an investment's return differs from the anticipated return, based around the historical norm. That is to say, how much the actual return deviates from the standard.

Let us consider an example.

Asset A is a high-risk share. On average it will grow by 10 per cent per annum, but the actual share price fluctuates quite wildly. As you can see from the chart below (diagram 10.1), the share price deviates quite substantially from the average annualised return.

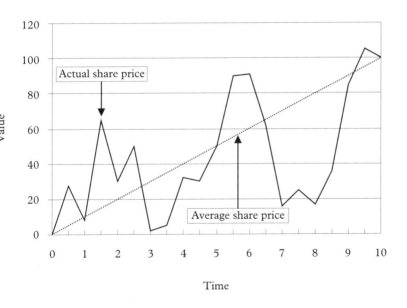

Diagram 10.1: Showing typical price pattern for a volatile share compared to average price.

The standard deviation is the amount by which the highs and lows deviate from the norm over a given period:

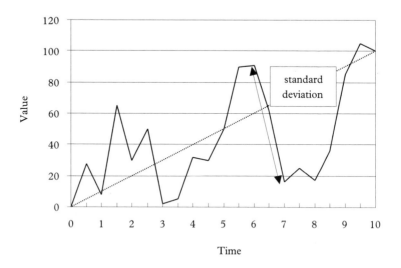

Diagram 10.2: Example of standard deviation measurement in a volatile asset.

Standard deviation is a useful measure because it shows us the risk or *variability of returns* of a particular asset over a chosen period. It can be very useful in comparing the nature of investment returns, where superficial data look similar. For example, in the marketing material of an investment company, two different funds are listed as follows:

Name of fund	Average annualised performance over 5 years
Risky Fund X	9 per cent per annum
Safe Fund Y	9 per cent per annum

On the face of it, these funds would *appear* to be offering the same return during a five-year period. And yet the way in which these returns were achieved differs greatly.

120

If you look at diagram 10.3, it is clear that Fund X is a lot riskier than Fund Y even if, looking backwards from today, they have both averaged about nine per cent per annum in arriving at their current valuation. But without knowing the standard deviation of each fund, an investor might buy Fund X expecting a *steady return* of 9 per cent per year, based on the figures given in the marketing literature, without realising that the next day his investment could drop by 30 per cent.

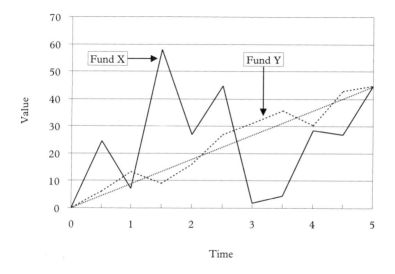

Diagram 10.3: Comparison of 'risky' asset with smooth return fund, both providing same average annual return over five years.

So, before entering into any investment, it is crucial to know the range of possible outcomes. The more these outcomes vary from what you require, the riskier the investment. Putting aside the risk of absolute loss, where a company goes bankrupt or your 'financial adviser' runs off with all your money, most outcomes will fall within a certain range of variations. And you can use standard deviation to measure this range.

Risk and reward

But risk by itself is only half the picture. The other half is reward. And the key to successful investing is to minimise the former, whilst maximising the latter.

An element of risk is necessary to achieve good returns. As we have shown throughout this book, reward demands risk, and it can take time to bear fruit. If we want to achieve higher than average returns, as most of us do, we will have to take some risks. But there is no point in taking pointless risks. *The key is to take on risk only to the extent that it can increase our chances of higher returns, and to avoid risk that won't.* But how do we know which is which? How do we know if investing in a particular asset, which contains an element of risk, is a good risk or a bad risk?

It was in pondering this dilemma that William Sharpe, a young finance professor in the business school at Washington University, came up with an idea that would measure both risk and return in the same formula. It was beautifully simple.

Sharpe idea!

The *Sharpe Ratio* is a way of expressing the return of an asset, adjusted to take into account the risk taken to achieve that return. It shows the return achieved for each measure of risk.

An asset with a high Sharpe Ratio shows it has achieved a high return relative to the risks taken to achieve that return. This is exactly what investors are looking for. By contrast, a low Sharpe Ratio means that the asset did not perform well relative to the risk taken, or it did not reward your higher risks with a higher return. One to avoid.

The Sharpe Ratio, then, expresses the return of an asset against how much risk, or how much volatility, it endured in order to achieve that return. It is calculated, broadly speaking, as the *return divided by the standard deviation.*

122

Let us give an example by comparing the share prices of Coca-Cola and Cisco over a period of one year. If the price of Coca-Cola shares went up by 10 per cent during the 12-month period, and displayed a standard deviation of 8 per cent, then a rough Sharpe Ratio for that period would be (10/8) = 1.25. By contrast, the share price of Cisco shares may have gone up by 12 per cent during the same period, but had a much higher standard deviation of 25 per cent. In this case, the Sharpe Ratio would have been 0.48 (12/25).

The higher number shows an asset that produces more return for each degree of risk. Accordingly, Coke shares were a better risk-adjusted investment during this period than Cisco. In order to achieve a marginally higher return (12 per cent) the Cisco shares had to endure a greatly exaggerated amount of volatility. Given that most investors want returns with minimal risk, the Coke shares were a better overall investment during this period.

Sharpe Ratios then are a great way of finding assets that perform well for the risk taken.

Armed with our understanding of standard deviation and Sharpe Ratios, we can now select assets that are likely to perform well given the level of volatility or risk we feel comfortable with. That means we can now find good individual investments.

But buying one share, or just one fund, no matter how carefully researched, is never a wise policy because all your money is too concentrated. Imagine if that asset, for whatever reason, were to fail. How would you cope then, if all your money were in that asset?

The next step in minimising your risk, then, is to diversify and build a winning mix of assets. As we saw in previous chapters, by diversifying across a range of different assets, we reduce our risk. This is because the possibility of loss affecting a wide range of different assets spread across different markets or sectors is much lower than if we had kept all our money in one asset.

123

But what is the best way to achieve this diversification? How do we know what to invest where? And what is the most suitable mix of assets for different investing goals?

Asset allocation

As we know, there are a number of basic asset classes: cash, bonds and shares. Each will have different profiles of risk and return. Asset allocation is the process of allocating different amounts of assets into different vehicles in such a blend as to meet your chosen goals in risk and return.

Asset allocation models can therefore help us decide *what proportion* of our investment to allocate to which asset class. For example, if you wanted to invest $10,000 and had a fairly conservative risk/return profile, you could use established asset allocation models to show yourself how much you should hold in cash, how much in bonds and how much in shares. These models tell you *how* to diversify.

Asset allocation models are useful in drawing up a basic portfolio model because different types of investment *behave* differently. That means the returns and the pattern of one asset type, such as cash, will differ from another type, such as shares.

Since we know that shares produce higher returns but tend to fluctuate more in value than cash, we can confidently predict that a portfolio with a *weighting* of 70 per cent shares and 30 per cent cash will tend to return more over time (but with greater volatility) than a portfolio with 50 per cent cash and only 50 per cent in shares. By varying the blend of different assets, the idea of using asset allocation models is to find a blend to suit yourself.

Studies show that asset allocation, even more than which actual shares or bonds you own, is *the most important determinant* of investment return. It is *how* you blend your assets, and the asset classes chosen, that will dictate your overall investment performance more than the actual companies or bonds you buy into.

124

The traditional benchmarks of asset allocation look something like this:

	Shares	Bonds	Cash
An aggressive portfolio:	70%	25%	5%
A balanced portfolio:	55%	30%	15%
A cautious portfolio:	30%	40%	30%

Standardised models such as the above table are a good place to start. They give us a general orientation to the sort of weightings a portfolio might have, according to conventional risk/return profiles.

However, there is a limit to the usefulness of these standardised models. While they are a good starting point, they offer only limited help in determining a real risk/return relationship in practise. Blanket terms such as conservative or cautious, balanced and aggressive, are all very well in theory but are too formulaic, too static. Investing should be about you, rather than a standardised set of boxes that you may or may not squeeze into. It is, after all, your money.

So, perhaps it's best to use the models above as a rough guide and then make the necessary adjustments to suit your own circumstances. You can then create a portfolio mix to meet your needs, rather than the other way around.

This takes us back to risk. You must control your risk, rather than allowing risk to control you. And it is here that the work of Harry Markowitz can help.

Modern portfolio theory and the efficient frontier

In 1950, while a young graduate student at Chicago University, Harry Markowitz changed the landscape of investing by introducing mathematical method to what had previously been something of a random art.

Markowitz knew that risk and return were inextricably

125

linked, and that to have more of one also meant having more of the other. He devised a simple graph to show this, with return on the vertical axis and risk (measured by standard deviation) on the horizontal axis.

Theoretically, the further you progress up the vertical axis (return), then the further you must also progress along the horizontal axis (risk). The more return you want, the more risk you'll have to take.

However, Markowitz knew that there must also be some investments that are better than others. That's to say there are some assets where you can take on less risk than others to achieve the same return. These are the sort of assets that investors should be looking for – where a higher return is achieved at the same degree of risk.

Consider the following graph:

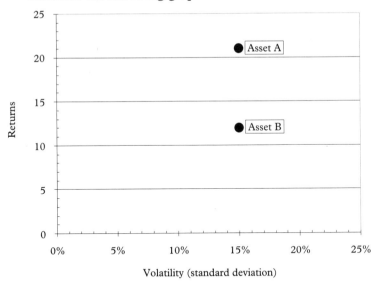

Diagram 10.4: Comparison between two assets with same volatility measure but different returns.

During a selected time period, asset A has produced a return of 21 per cent with a standard deviation of 15 per

126

cent. Asset B, by contrast, produced only 12 per cent for the same level of volatility. Clearly, asset A is a better investment than asset B. For the same degree of risk, in other words, asset A returned almost double the return of asset B.

If there was no other asset producing a better return with this level of volatility than asset A (ie no other asset could be plotted vertically above asset A on the chart), then A clearly provides the best possible return at this level of risk. It is the optimum, or most efficient, asset.

Markowitz went on to explore this further. He wanted to discover the optimum asset at each point along the risk axis – meaning the asset giving the highest possible return at each level of risk.

He did this by plotting the risk and return profiles of hundreds of different assets onto a graph like the one opposite. And what he found led to the creation of one of the key concepts in modern portfolio theory – the efficient frontier.

By plotting these various points, and joining the lines together, the most efficient assets at each point formed an optimum risk/return curve, tracing a swooping arc from top right to centre left.

Because these assets represent the optimum or most-efficient return for each specific degree of risk, and because the line they trace forms a frontier that cannot be passed by any other known investment, Markowitz named this curve the *efficient frontier.* Any asset lying on the efficient frontier provides, by definition, the highest return for that particular level of risk.

His next step was to consider how this could be applied to the blending of different stand-alone assets to create an investment portfolio. He knew, intuitively, that by having a mix of assets rather than just one he would be reducing his risk. The real question was less whether or not to diversify, but rather *how* to diversify most efficiently to achieve the highest-possible return with the lowest-overall risk.

Markowitz's answer to this question has become one of the foundations of modern portfolio theory. He found that the best results arrived when he constructed portfolios of assets that were *unrelated* to each other.

We've seen before how it makes sense to buy a range of assets rather than just one in order to reduce the risk of a large loss affecting one of your assets. However, this approach is no good if all your assets are invested in the same field or sector.

If you diversify your holdings across many types of unrelated investments you reduce the risk that they will all tumble in value at once. Thus, as Markowitz said, unrelated investments smooth investment returns: "you've got to look at the portfolio as a whole, not just position by position. And if you're trying to reduce the volatility or uncertainty of your portfolio, then you need more than one (share) obviously, but you also need (shares) that don't go up and down together."

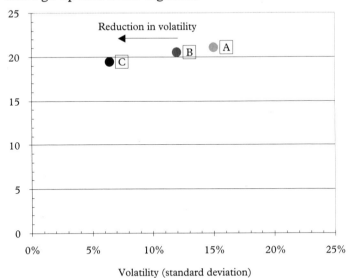

Diagram 10.5: A comparison of risk and return profiles for an idividual share (A), a mix of similar shares (B) and a portfolio of unrelated shares (C).

Consider the example on the opposite page. Point A represents the risk/return profile of a single asset, for example a share in Coca-Cola. It produces a good return, but the risk is quite high. Point B represents the risk/return profile of a portfolio of 10 shares, all within the soft drinks sector – risk has been reduced, from 15 per cent to 12 per cent, but it is still quite high. This is because the assets, while individually diversified, are all in the same sector, namely soft drinks. The best overall position is Point C, which is the risk/return profile of a portfolio comprising ten unrelated shares. The risk at point C has been significantly reduced with little or no reduction in performance compared to A or B. Of all the choices open to investors, C represents the best compromise between risk and reward.

This was revolutionary. Not only had Markowitz mathematically proven the benefits of diversification in optimising investment returns but he'd also laid out a template for the scientific blending of different assets to improve returns and reduce risk. And he'd shown that for diversification really to work, assets had to be uncorrelated.

If you look at diagram 10.6 on the next page, the optimum blend is the data point closest to the left, where the highest possible return also meets the lowest possible risk. This is a real example of how adding an uncorrelated asset class, managed futures (discussed later in this chapter), to a typical mix of shares and bonds improves the possibility for performance while lowering overall volatility. For investors wishing to base their portfolios around bonds and shares, this is the portfolio allocation to aim for.

The lasting achievement of Markowitz was to prove not only that risk could be reduced through diversification but also to show how the risk/return relationship could be analysed, plotted and almost manufactured. This laid the foundations for the tremendous explosion of the fund management industry in the 1970s and 1980s – where professional money managers could at last follow a systematic way to achieve growth while minimising risk.

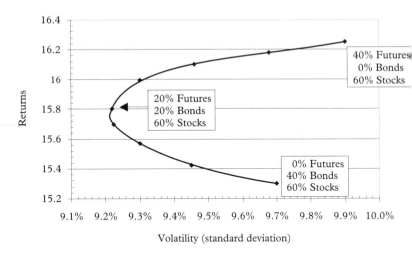

Diagram 10.6: Effect of adding managed futures to mix of non-correlated assets to minimise volatility and improve returns. Based upon monthly data 1980–1998, stocks are S&P 500 (dividends reinvested); bonds are US long-term bonds; and managed futures are MAR Fund/Qualified Universe Index.

Markowitz wasn't the first to suggest the link between risk, return and diversification, he simply made the relationship more quantifiable.

As we have seen, Sharpe and Markowitz revolutionised the field of investment through the application of scientific method. The tools they helped develop, and the various portfolio theories that grew out of them, are popular across the world, from amateurs with a couple of thousand dollars to invest, to institutions managing billions.

In 1990, for 'their pioneering work in the theory of financial economics,' Harry Markowitz and William Sharpe were awarded the Nobel Prize for Economics.

A summary of risk-reduction tools

As we've seen, we can use standard deviation and the Sharpe Ratio to help select assets that give us what we want (and minimise nasty surprises) and we can use diversification, asset allocation and the efficient frontier to blend different assets in such a way as to further minimise overall risk.

Using these tools, we address the first part of successful investing – minimising our risk. Now we can turn our attention to ways of maximising our growth.

In the next few pages, you'll find some suggestions on how best to invest in the three main asset classes you're likely to come across as an expat: shares, equity-based mutual funds and alternative investment funds.

1. Making money from shares

In chapter seven we explained how shares work and how they can make money for you. Now we'll give you some practical tips on maximising your growth potential with shares.

First of all, you need to decide how you intend to invest. When you invest in shares, you can invest either for the short term or for the longer term.

Short-term investing means getting in and out of the market quickly, with the intention of making a fast profit from a rise in share prices. It can yield spectacular results but it carries high risks. You are betting that you either know more than other market observers or you have a hunch that turns out to be lucky. Since it's highly unlikely you'll have more access to information than professional stock-market traders, your greatest hope here is luck. And luck is a temporary guest.

Returns come easily in a bull market (when prices are rising). When everybody wants to get in on the share circus, it doesn't take a great deal of skill to make money. Shares are only going in one direction (upwards) and there are plenty of other investors willing to buy your shares, regardless of whether they represent a good deal or not. This drives prices up further.

But a rising market doesn't last forever. When the bubble bursts, and it always does, anyone still in the market will lose money. It can be a long and painful process to recover. Some speculators never do recover – remember day-traders in the year 2000? – and remember how difficult it can be, or how long it can take, to regain your position once you've made a loss?

Making money from share speculation is more like gambling, rather than investing. As with any gambling, if you are going to play, only play with money you can afford to lose. And if you get a lucky break, don't fool yourself – you're not an expert or investment guru. You've been lucky, that's all.

If you invest for the *longer-term*, by contrast, you should aim to buy a co-ownership in great companies in whose profits you want to share. There is some skill involved as you'll need to do your research and make intelligent decisions.

This is how the world's best-known investors make their money. It is through careful analysis and a long-term view. Above all, they see themselves as buying a *part-ownership* in the companies they invest in, rather than simply buying shares on a stock market. As such, they are more inclined to do their homework before choosing to invest in a particular company. It is a business decision, after all.

One of the world's leading investors is an American called Warren Buffet. He tends to buy long-term holdings in steady, well-managed companies. He will often opt for companies paying *good dividends* – these, if you recall from chapter seven, are the annual share of the company's profits. And what do good dividends tell us? That the company is being well managed and its products are in demand.

Do not overlook the significance of dividends. The world seems obsessed with chasing the mirage of growth, the ever-fluctuating rise (and fall) of share prices. But a share price is only what someone else, called the market, thinks it's worth. The market may be right or it may be wrong – it is purely a matter of opinion.

But a dividend, by contrast, is cash. And cash is real.

When all the sound and fury surrounding share prices disappears during the hangover of a bear market, cash is king. This is when dividends, and companies paying dividends, are at their most attractive. And when a company's share is attractive, other investors will want a piece of the action, creating a demand that drives prices upwards.

A smart investor with a long-term view will tend to buy companies paying steady dividends and then, particularly in the lows, use those dividends to buy more shares in that company. He knows that those shares are likely to rebound in value before too long.

Buying for the long term, choosing great companies paying solid dividends, and then reinvesting the dividends. It is a simple strategy and it works.

2. Making money from managed funds

Managed funds, mainly of the type known as mutual funds, are now the most popular way to invest in the financial markets around the world. These funds are a good way to get started in investment, since they provide a convenient way into a wide range of markets and enjoy an inherent risk reduction through their diversification.

However, there are plenty to choose from. So how would you go about choosing the best fund?

The answer is *with difficulty*. Each mutual-fund company will have a marketing department whose job it is to persuade you that their fund is the best in its sector and easily out-performs its rivals. Their brief is to show their funds in the best possible light, even if that means selective use of data or invalid comparisons. It's up to you to try and find the truth behind the marketing gloss.

This is not always easy. For example, most companies will trumpet their past performance in order to sell their funds. And yet they will write in the small print that 'past performance is not necessarily a guide to future returns' or some such disclaimer. On the one hand they are using past performance to promote their funds, then they are telling you that it has nothing to do with what might happen in the future!

The reality is that, over any quantifiable period, past performance has very little bearing on the future performance of an investment fund. Short-term returns have more to do with luck than skill and if a fund manager does show demonstrable skill, he is easily lured away to another investment company paying more. What percentage of fund managers do you think stay with one investment company for more than five years?

The answer is six per cent.

. . . I'd like to introduce our star fund manager . . .

So, trying to compare funds based upon past performance is a rather fruitless exercise.

Rather than spending a lot of time and energy trying to find which fund is 'better' than the others using historical data, it makes more sense to simply spread your funds across a range of different providers. Some will be winners, some losers, but at least you have spread your risk. If you want to invest in the European markets, for example, choose three or four providers offering these funds rather than just one. And choose institutions you feel comfortable with, offering strategies that suit you and with *low-expense ratios*, rather than looking at how they performed in the last 10 years.

One alternative, of course, is to forget the idea of active fund management altogether. Many investors are now finding that they could be better off in an *index fund*.

Index funds are a relatively new phenomenon. They are popular among savers and investors who want to diversify and harness the growth of stock markets but don't necessarily want to pay for a fund manager.

An index fund invests your money in all the stocks and shares of companies making up a major market index, such as the US Dow Jones index or the UK's FTSE 100. The majority of these funds (also called *tracker* funds) will simply invest in all the stocks on that market, and their performance will therefore *track* the performance of the index as a whole.

By the very nature of the index, which only lists the top companies on that particular market, the companies making up your fund will tend to be winners – any poorly performing company will automatically drop out of the index and thus out of the fund. To a degree, an index fund will tend to manage itself, without needing a fund manager as such.

The beauty of an index fund is that, by doing away with the active management of a fund manager, you also do away with many of the costs associated with managed funds. A growing body of evidence also shows that these passively-managed funds actually *outperform* actively-managed funds.

Index funds are a good base for any long-term fund portfolio and it's a good idea to have one for each major market sector you wish to participate in, as much for the cost savings as anything else. Having said that, because there's no active management to smooth investment performance by blending shares with cash or bonds, an index fund will tend to provide a bumpier ride than a typical managed fund. If you can deal with this emotionally and financially, then go ahead and invest in index trackers.

On the other hand, if you still prefer to have active management, but want to diversify away from just shares or market indices, perhaps you should also consider the growing range of alternative-investment vehicles now available to expats.

3. Investing in alternative-investment vehicles

Traditional mutual funds, whether actively managed or not, will invest in cash, bonds and shares, with the emphasis on the latter to generate much of the growth.

Alternative investment funds, by contrast, will invest in a much wider universe of underlying assets, and employ a range of investing techniques in order to make money, rather than just buying in the hope that prices will go up.

An alternative investment fund will typically invest in options, futures, warrants, and other sophisticated financial instruments (known collectively as *derivatives*) that are derived from basic stock-market vehicles. As many of these funds aim to make money in falling as well as rising markets, thereby 'hedging your bets', they're known as *hedge funds*.

Hedge funds are big business. There are approximately 600 hedge funds available internationally, with more than six-trillion US dollars invested. This is the equivalent of

$1,000 for every person on the planet.

On their own, the individual assets into which these funds invest can be very risky. Buying options, futures or commodities is not something for a novice investor. However, by blending together a range of different assets – and different strategies – a typical managed hedge fund could offer a reasonably acceptable risk profile and good opportunities for growth.

Many of these funds, unlike mutual funds, can also *go short* (sell shares they do not own in the hope of buying them later at a lower price) and use borrowed money to make big growth from small price changes (called *leverage*). The net effect of these techniques is that hedge funds can *make money* in a flat or even falling market, as well as a rising market.

Because the assets they invest in and the techniques they use (going short, for example) differ from traditional investment funds, having a hedge fund in your portfolio can significantly reduce overall risk while also increasing the overall potential for return. Look again at the graph in diagram 10.6 showing the introduction of a hedge fund to a portfolio previously based just on shares and bonds.

However, you do need to be doubly sure about your risk exposure with these types of funds. Many are marketed as low-risk products, or designed to appeal to investors looking for capital security, but this can be misleading. They can also be difficult to understand fully, so it's well worth while taking qualified and independent guidance if you're thinking of investing this way.

Alternative investments don't just have to mean hedge funds, though. An alternative investment is anything that diversifies away from the traditional asset classes of cash, bonds and shares, whether bundled together as a fund or not.

Alternative investments can also mean precious metals, such as gold or platinum. Gold in particular is popular among many expats from the Indian subcontinent as it can

137

be worn and enjoyed as well as holding its value. Other alternative investments could be works of art, commodities such as coffee beans, commercial real estate, even vintage cars, all of which have, at one time or another, provided the opportunity for explosive growth.

Strange though it may seem, people have become millionaires by trading in such unglamorous commodities as soya beans or processed meat products. In the search for good investments, it pays to keep an open mind.

A final word about investing in funds

Before you invest into any collective investment scheme, though, it is vital to do your research. Check the declared strategy of each fund or investment product and see that it suits you. If you are a cautious investor looking at managed funds, check that the fund's prospectus shows how the manager intends to manage risk. If there's a target Sharpe Ratio, then study this and compare it with other funds.

And be sure to check what protection you have if things go wrong. Look for regulatory approval from a credible offshore centre – funds regulated in the Isle of Man, Luxembourg, Switzerland, Guernsey and Jersey are usually well-structured and legitimate. To be on the safe side, it's worth checking on any compensation or investor protection schemes operating in the relevant territory.

Fraud happens, and bogus funds are all too common. Just make sure you don't invest in one of them.

The importance of playing bridge

Our last observation is the simplest. It also requires the least amount of work: in fact, the less you do, the better.

The 17th century French philosopher Blaise Pascal once wrote, "All man's miseries derive from not being able to sit quietly in a room alone." And how well this applies to investing. . . .

One of the greatest, and most dangerous, temptations you'll face once you start managing your money is the feeling that you ought to be doing something with it every day.

The danger here is obvious. Not only do you massively push up your transaction costs, with all your frantic buying and selling, but you can also sell out prematurely from good holdings, where all you needed was a little time for the growth to come through.

Successful investing demands the patience and discipline to make big bets during the relatively infrequent intervals when the markets are undervalued, and the self-control to do 'something else' during the long periods when markets are fully priced or overpriced.

Warren Buffett, as always, sums it up nicely. Successful investing does not require superior intelligence or fancy mathematical tools – it simply requires diligence, discipline and patience: "once you have ordinary intelligence, what you need is the temperament to control the urges that get other people into trouble when investing."

Remember, buy good assets at good prices, and hold on to them. Find something else to do when the markets are overpriced, even if this means not doing anything with your investments for a long time. In 1970, Buffett was so concerned at high prices in the stock market that he stopped making new investments for a full four years. It was only in 1974, famously comparing the low market prices to a "harem filled with beautiful women," that he made another new purchase. And during that time, what was the 'something else' he was busying himself with?

Apparently, he was playing a lot of bridge!

Advanced investing – a summary

We've tried to give you some generic tools in this chapter and some ideas for strategies that you might find useful.

Of course, nothing here is specific advice, you have to make your own mind up and make your own decisions.

A basic guidebook on financial planning is not the place to find detailed answers on how you should invest. But we hope some of the ideas have been helpful. As a reminder:

1. *Always* do your preparation.
2. Research and learn to use risk-reduction tools for yourself.
3. Control your costs (transaction costs and taxes where relevant).
4. Don't confuse information with knowledge!
5. Diversify.
6. Review on a set timeframe.
7. Be realistic.
8. . . . and have patience.

Chapter eleven

Case studies

Let's put all of the theory behind us and see how it works in real life. In this final chapter, we've invented some typical expat characters, both single and with families, to demonstrate how financial planning can be used to achieve your goals in life.

In each case, the characters tell us about themselves, their circumstances, their dreams and how they currently manage their finances (or not!). We then draw up a list of suggestions for them to consider, aiming towards an integrated financial plan for each. By now, you should be able to predict what most of these suggestions will be, before you read them. Why not try it, as a test?

Young, free and single

Pieter is 24 years old and has recently arrived in the Gulf from South Africa. He is very ambitious and wants to be a millionaire at 40!

One of the problems he experienced in South Africa was the depreciation of his currency. Now he's living internationally, he doesn't want that to happen again, so he's committed to building up his funds in a hard currency – in this case US dollars.

Having heard about fortunes being made on the stock market, he wants to invest everything he has there, right now. He figures that, by the time he's 40, he should have enough from his investments to spend the rest of his life at leisure.

He has just bought himself the Jeep he always wanted, which used up all of his savings. He's also thinking about buying a property to rent in his home city of Cape Town.

Prices are very low by international standards, and he thinks this could be a good investment.

What should he do?

Foundations: First things first. Pieter may be keen to invest in the stock market, but he has no emergency buffer and no insurance. His first priorities would be to check his insurances (particularly medical cover, which he was accustomed to back home), and then to build up his emergency savings fund. He shouldn't do anything with his money until his buffer covers at least three month's salary. As he likes the outdoor life, and enjoys playing sport, he should also look at an income-replacement plan that will cover his income if he cannot work because of a sports injury.

Allocating disposable income: Once this is done, he can start saving regular amounts of money into the stock market, through a mixture of managed funds, index funds, and individual stocks. For the first few years, he will limit his personal involvement in selecting the investments, choosing instead to invest through collective funds. This will give him time to learn about stock market investing for himself.

He should also think carefully about the idea of buying a property in Cape Town. If he isn't planning to return there, the house is an investment property and not a home. As such, he needs to distance himself from the emotional motives behind buying a house in his hometown, and treat it simply as a business decision. The two are quite separate.

The 'just marrieds'

Khalil is a Canadian citizen, whose family emigrated there from Lebanon when he was three years old. He's recently married Maya, from Beirut, and they have settled in the Gulf. They want to end up in Canada but are happy to stay where they are for the next five to eight years.

Their particular challenge is financial discipline – they simply don't have any! Despite each of them earning high salaries, there's nothing left at the end of the month. And, what's worse, they have no idea where it all goes.

Their joint spending habits mean that they also have around $5,000 debt on a mixture of credit cards. Although they think they are paying the cards off every month, the balance never seems to fall.

As they both work for multi-national companies, their life, medical and disability insurances are paid for by their employers. However, Khalil may not stay with his current employer for long. They also plan to start a family in the next two or three years, as they think this is a good place to raise a young family.

How will they achieve their dreams?

Make a plan: Their first priority is to wake up and take a good look at their financial situation, starting with their spending habits. Both need to do an income/expenditure review. They will probably find that his love for expensive cars and her weakness for jewellery have something to do with their financial situation.

Manage debt: Their next priority is to manage the debt on their credit cards. When they look into it further, they may well discover that they are both paying the minimum balance only on each card and that's why they never seem to bring the balance down. They should commit to paying regular lump sums to clear the balance owing, and then set up a regular instruction to clear the cards in full at the end of each month.

Start saving: Once they've completed their income and expenditure analysis, they realise how much of their potential future wealth is being wasted on things they can do without. So, they should both set a monthly budget and agree to save a fixed amount on a regular basis. Having done their sums, they realise that they can both put away at least $1,000 each per month. They agree to put this into the bank for the time being, rather than

143

getting stuck on some complicated investment strategy. Their challenge is simply to get into the habit of saving. If they manage to do this, and there is a lump sum in the bank in a year's time, they will then consider a mix of places to invest their regular savings. Maya prefers security, Khalil likes a bit of adventure, but that is a discussion to have a year down the road, not now. **Insurance:** Khalil's future employers may not be as generous as his current ones with regard to employee benefits, so he should do his research on buying their own insurance plans, particularly if they are planning to start a family soon. The quicker they get working on their foundations, the better. When looking at medical insurance, in particular, it would be a good idea to choose a plan from an international provider that can be transferred to a Canadian provider when they finally emigrate.

The young family

Rajesh and Geetha are both from India. He is 35 and she is 27. They have two children, Ashok (three) and Deepa (one).

As Rajesh is a doctor, from a family of doctors, and Geetha practices law, they want their children to have the very best start in life, having learnt the value of education for themselves. They hope that Ashok and Deepa will follow in their footsteps to become lawyers or doctors. Geetha often jokes that they should become both – solicitors specialising in medical law!

For Rajesh and Geetha, this head start means two things: international schooling, in the Gulf and the UK, followed by university in the States.

But, so far, they've failed to do anything concrete for their children. Rajesh has been 'too busy' to look at life insurance, so they have none, and they don't really know what schools and universities in the West are likely to cost.

How can they be sure they are doing the right thing for Ashok and Deepa?

Protection: Before planning their children's education fees it is important they consider life insurance to ensure that the children can continue their studies if anything happens to either parent. They decide to set up a monthly insurance plan, which will pay $200,000 in the event of their death whilst the children are under 18. This should be enough to meet the schooling fees for each child.

Education fees: Rajesh and Geetha then need to work out a fees schedule, to calculate the likely cost of school and university. They could use the Internet to search for information on typical school and university fees. Once they know the cost, they can establish how much they need to set aside on a monthly basis. Such a schedule could look like this:

Period from present	Year	Opening balance	Regular investment each year	End value after 8% net growth	Child one fees (Ashok)	Child two fees (Deepa)	End balance
1	2004	0	6,607	6,835			6,835
2	2005	6,835	6,937	14,556			14,556
3	2006	14,556	7,284	23,249			23,249
4	2007	23,249	7,648	33,011			33,011
5	2008	33,011	8,031	43,946			43,946
6	2009	43,946	8,432	56,165			56,165
7	2010	56,165	8,854	69,793			69,793
8	2011	69,793	9,297	84,963			84,963
9	2012	84,963	9,761	101,820			101,820
10	2013	101,820	10,249	120,523			120,523
11	2014	120,523	10,762	141,245			141,245
12	2015	141,245	11,300	164,171			164,171
13	2016	164,171	11,865	189,506			189,506
14	2017	189,506	12,458	217,470			217,470
15	2018	217,470	13,081	248,303	45,398		202,925
16	2019	202,925	0	219,068	46,739		172,329
17	2020	172,329	0	186,037	48,141	48,141	89,755
18	2021	89,755	0	96,895		49,585	47,310
19	2022	47,310	0	51,073		51,073	0
20	2023	0	0	0			0

Diagram 11.1: Table showing the planning of schools fees, assuming 8 per cent growth each year, increasing the contribution by 5 per cent every year over 15 years

Having worked out how much they need to save, they then need to discuss where to allocate the money. Rajesh is an accountant, so he understands the principle of risk and return and its relationship with time. Given that their time horizon is relatively long, they decide upon a mixed basket of funds and shares, which blends secure return investments with some more aggressive opportunities.
Retirement: Difficult though it is, with all their other expenses, this is also prime time for Rajesh and Geetha to build funds for their later years. Rajesh has a couple of houses in Bangalore, which provide a good rental income and have appreciated in value quite considerably. He is also building a separate savings fund, in dollars, for himself and Geetha. Having sold out of the stock market when it reached its peak some years previously, making some very good gains in the process, this money is currently sitting in a bank, earning a rather pitiful interest. Rajesh is happy to let it stay there for a while. When he sees a good opportunity, he's going to invest again, probably drip-feeding the money into funds and shares to even out any short-term volatility.

The 'perpetual bachelor'

Michael is 47 years old and completely broke.

Since his divorce two years ago, he has had to pick himself up and start again. Leaving the UK and coming to the Gulf was a good move, as he should be able to save seriously, but other amusements have kept getting in his way. As a result he hasn't made the progress he was hoping to.

In fact, he has absolutely nothing to his name: no house, no savings and no insurance. Someone told him he would be looked after by the state when he retires, but he's beginning to doubt this. Another acquaintance told him he should invest in a property-based savings scheme, but he isn't so sure – he'd never heard of the company. He doesn't know what to do, whether to buy a house, get a pension plan, or simply keep whatever he can save under the mattress?

He wants to stop working by the time he is 65, but doesn't know if he can. Where does he start?

Get saving: Mike's key priority is his retirement. In just over 15 years, he's going to stop work and who's going to support him then? He needs to get serious about his financial life, and take some control. He won't have another opportunity like this again.

His first step is to check with the state benefits department in the UK about his entitlement to a state pension. He will be shocked to learn that he'll only receive the equivalent of $30 a week, from age 65 – about $1,500 a year – because of his intermittent contributions to social security.

He then needs to sit down and work out how to build his own pot, by himself. Given that he wants to stop working full-time at age 65 on about one half of his current income, he should do some rough calculations on how much he needs to save. Assuming a seven per cent growth rate on his retirement assets, he needs to put away approximately $ 1,500 per month.

This will mean some serious discipline with his disposable income. But, as he grudgingly admits, he doesn't really have much choice. He knows that he has a chance to get back on his feet again now and he'd be a fool to miss this opportunity. The alternative is not worth thinking about.

Protection: Having lost most of his assets once before in his life, Mike doesn't want that to happen again. As a safeguard, he's taking the wise step of insuring his health and his income to protect his retirement fund.

The 'have-it-alls'

If Mike's problem was having nothing to his name, Donald and Mary are the complete opposite. Their challenge, if not exactly having too much to their names, is working out how best to manage all the assets they've accumulated.

They have been in the Gulf for 20 years. He's 57 and she is 55. Donald is the CEO of a very successful business he started some 15 years ago with a local partner. Mary runs a home furnishing business, which is very profitable even though she only started it to keep herself occupied.

Both their children are financially independent, having set up their own businesses in different parts of the world and started their own families some time ago.

Donald and Mary have a substantial portfolio of stocks and shares being handled by a well-known private banking firm. Although it did quite well during the 1990s, for the past few years the portfolio has been making losses every year. When he last looked, the portfolio was heavily invested in speculative and aggressive shares, which concerned Donald.

In a few years' time, they intend to leave the Gulf and return to Europe. They have a large house in central Dublin, which is their main home. They also have a house in the south of France where they plan to spend their winters, being somewhat warmer than Dublin.

From that point forward, their share portfolio, and the money from selling their businesses, will be their only income. Sounds idyllic, but what hidden dangers will they face?

Business: The key challenge facing Donald and Mary is to protect the wealth they've built up. Firstly, they have to divest themselves of their business assets over the forthcoming years, ensuring that they achieve a good price for what they've built up. They then need to think carefully about how to invest this wisely, to sustain them in the years ahead.

Investment allocation: They need to be sure that their current and future investment portfolio is suitable for their stage of life – a heavy weighting towards aggressive and speculative shares might not be very appropriate for them right now, when all they need is income. Their portfolio should be re-balanced to reflect this, with a greater emphasis on secure assets, paying a smooth and regular income.

Tax planning: They need to think about the tax consequences of what they do, and what they own. It will pay to take specific tax advice now, before taking any action. Living in France and Ireland will certainly give rise to tax on their substantial income. They need to think about ways to mitigate this, through structuring their investment income in the most tax-efficient way. They might also look into which jurisdiction offers the more favourable regime, and see if they can spend more time there. They need to get working on their estate planning as soon as possible, to ensure that their wealth can be preserved for their children. And, if they haven't made a will, they should make an appointment with their lawyer this afternoon!

Some final words

These examples may be a little simplistic, but they make the point. Your finances, particularly how you handle them, have a large role to play in determining the outcome, and the very enjoyment, of your life.

Your money is rather like your health in this regard. If there are two things that really affect the course of your life, and over which you have some degree of control, it's money and health. It's worth thinking about this for a while.

Like your health, you have to look after your money, even work at it sometimes, to make the most of it. Like your health, finding a balance with your money is vital: being over-zealous can be as damaging as doing nothing. And like your health, the bulk of the responsibility for your financial well-being starts and finishes with you.

Money can't buy happiness, for sure, but it can give you choice. How you use that choice, of course, is up to

149

you – but choice, as a gift in itself, is a wonderful thing.

As an expat, you have an opportunity that may not last forever. It's your choice whether or not you want to make the most of it. If you do – and we hope you do if you've reached this far in the book – here are some final tips:

Pay particular attention to getting your *foundation* right. Virtually everything that you (and your family) currently enjoy depends on you being alive, healthy and able to work. Address your protection before anything else – for your family's sake if not for yours.

Think carefully about how best to use your *disposable income*. You must set some of it aside if you are going to have anything later in life, particularly as an expat, where your home country is even less than normally inclined to look after you. By all means enjoy your current lifestyle, but don't consume everything.

Allocate future money according to when you might need it, what returns you expect to gain, and how you deal with ups-and-downs in the short-term value.

Get serious about *retirement* income as soon as you can. Think less about 'pensions' and more about funding your own private income for the time after paid regular employment. Think less about being 'retired' and more about being 'financially independent'.

Invest wisely – treat investing like a business decision. Diversify, have patience and be realistic.

Above all, try and make the most of the opportunity you have right now.

The road to financial security makes for an interesting journey, and it starts as soon as you close this book. Good luck and *bon voyage*!

Acknowledgements

Many people have been instrumental in enabling this book to be written and published.

My thanks go first of all to the numerous individuals and companies throughout the Gulf who have been kind enough to listen to my advice, even to the extent of following it from time to time! This book has its origins in the countless discussions we've had on the best way to manage money whilst living in the Gulf region and how to be a successful investor in these complex times.

In addition, I would like to express my thanks to Harry Holt, through whom I became interested in investment theory, the staff of Motivate Publishing for their hard work in preparing the book for publication, Julian Raymond and Nick Earles of Kingstar Insurance Agencies LLC in Dubai for their sponsorship, Haroon Mahmood of MiNC Property Enterprises for his expert counsel on property investing, JC for his wonderful cartoons, and my wife Nadine for her ongoing support.

Robin Wells, Dubai, April 2004

Life, Medical and Employee Benefits Specialists